Keep Cool!

Berufsvorbereitung Englisch

von
Birgit Herrmann
Andrew K. Johnson

Ernst Klett Verlag
Stuttgart · Leipzig

Keep Cool! im Englischunterricht

Das komplett überarbeitete Keep Cool! ist für Schülerinnen und Schüler in berufsvorbereitenden Schulen (BVJ, BEK, BGJ, Einstiegsschulen) und trainiert alle geforderten Kompetenzen auf dem Einstiegsniveau (A1). In außerschulischen Kursen ist Keep Cool! ebenfalls der ideale Start für junge Erwachsene, die wenige oder keine Vorkenntnisse in Englisch haben.

1. Neuerungen auf einen Blick

- **Komplette Neubearbeitung** der Schülerbuch-Inhalte, der Konzeption und des Layouts
- Im Mittelpunkt aller Units steht die **Kommunikation im (Berufs-)Alltag**; dabei liegt die Betonung auf dem Verständnis von gesprochenem und geschriebenem Englisch.
- Unterschiedliche Schülerkenntnisse erfordern starke **Differenzierung**:
  - nach unten durch multimediale und interaktive Online-Übungsaufgaben (*Üben interaktiv*)
  - nach oben durch Auswahlmöglichkeiten zwischen verschieden schweren **1** und **2** Aufgaben, berufsrelevante *Jobsites* oder Vokabeltrainingseiten.
  - weitere Aufgaben und Hilfen zur Differenzierung im Lehrerhandbuch.
- Motivierendes **Multimedia-Training**:
  - Download des **Talking Vocabulary** als MP3-Daten über die Keep Cool!-Codes zu Beginn jeder Unit.
  - 7 **BBC-Videos** zum Training des Seh-Hörverstehens. Dabei wird das authentische Material durch grafische Vokabelhinweise zum leichteren Verstehen entlastet.
- **Grammatik** wird in kleinen Einheiten wiederholt und geübt.
- **Vokabeltraining** pur:
  - Vor allem **jobrelevante Vokabeln** werden – neben der Wiederholung des Grundwortschatzes – sukzessive eingeführt und trainiert.
  - Da die Vokabeln bereits auf jeder Seite erklärt werden, sind die **Vokabeltrainingseiten** (*Vocabulary*) im Anhang konzentriert auf das jeweilige Thema mit begleitenden Vokabelübungen.
  - Über den Keep Cool!-Code kann ein **Compact dictionary** Deutsch – Englisch kostenlos heruntergeladen werden.

2. So sind die Units aufgebaut

- Einstiegsdoppelseite **Entry/Audio**: Vorbereitung auf das jeweilige Lehrplanthema durch interessante Bildmotive bzw. humorvolle Hörverstehensaufgaben.
- Doppelseite **Text** übt das Leseverstehen – mit eingebettetem Skills-Training.
- 2 Seiten **Interaction** bereiten im Besonderen auf die mündlichen und schriftlichen Kompetenzen in der Praxis vor.
- **Anhang – Keep Cool! tools**
  - **Job-Seiten** vermitteln die wichtigste Lexik attraktiver Berufe.
  - **Vokabeltrainingseiten** bündeln thematisch die wichtigsten Vokabeln, begleitet von Übungen, zuzüglich Grundwortschatz und alphabetischem Vokabular.
  - **Video lounge** stellt Aufgaben zu den BBC-Videos zur Verfügung.
  - **Klappumschläge** bieten wichtiges Sprachmaterial wie Phrases, Zeitformen, etc. auf einen Blick.

3. Variante Cool!

Cool! ist die Alternative, um Schülerinnen und Schüler auf den nachgeholten bzw. verbesserten Hauptschulabschluss vorzubereiten (A2).

Lernhilfen

Ziel:	Lernzielformulierungen: Ich weiß, warum ich das lerne.
Vocabulary:	Vokabelfokus
Grammar:	Grammatikfokus
flat Wohnung	Vokabelerläuterungen in der Randspalte
2	anspruchsvolle Aufgabe

Symbole

A1.12	Hörverstehensaufgabe oder Lesetext, Track 12 auf Audio-CD 1 im Lehrerhandbuch
◉ V1	Original BBC-Video
 f6en95	Keep Cool!-Codes: kostenlos unter www.klett.de 1. Downloads: Talking vocabulary (vertonte Wortlisten) als MP3-Daten, Keep Cool! compact dictionary (die komplette Wortliste Deutsch – Englisch) 2. Üben interaktiv: Multimediale Online-Aufgaben zu Differenzierung und Selbststudium
Example	Beispiele, Musterlösungen
⟶ G1	Verweise auf die Grammatik im Anhang

Inhalt

1 Turn me on

Ziel: Ich kann sagen, was ich regelmäßig mache. *Beispiel: I listen to music.*

What are Carlo's and Ella's hobbies?
Was sind Carlos und Ellas Hobbys?

*Hi. I'm Carlo.
My hobby is music.
I listen to music
all the time.
I'm a hip-hop fan.*

*This is Ella, my younger sister.
She likes music too.
She often uses her smartphone.
She likes pop.*

A **1** **What do you think? Who likes Nicki Minaj and Eminem?**
Was glauben Sie? Wem gefallen Nicki Minaj und Eminem?

_____

2 **And who likes Katy Perry and Justin Bieber?**
Und wer mag Katy Perry und Justin Bieber?

_____

Vocabulary: Über Hobbys sprechen

cook, dance, do sport, go shopping, hang out with friends, read, surf the internet, watch TV

to turn on
einschalten, anmachen

all the time
die ganze Zeit

to hang out
„abhängen"

to surf the internet
im Internet surfen

favourite
Lieblings-

singer
Sänger/in

B **What about you?**
Und Sie?

I like _____

_____

My favourite singer/group is _____

A bad day for BigDadDave

A **Listen to the story. Tick the right picture (1 or 2).**

A2.1 Hören Sie sich die Geschichte an. Machen Sie ein Häkchen an das passende Bild (1 oder 2).

B **Listen to the story again. Tick *true* or *false* for sentences 1–4.**
Hören Sie sich die Geschichte noch einmal an. Machen Sie bei den Sätzen 1–4 ein Häkchen bei *richtig* oder *falsch*.

	true	false
1 Dave is a rapper.	☐	☐
2 Dave works in a music shop.	☐	☐
3 Dave is usually good at his job.	☐	☐
4 Mary is Dave's mother.	☐	☐

Grammar: to be (= sein) ⟶ G7

I am	I'm
you are	you're
he/she/it is	he's/she's/it's
we are	we're
you are	you're
they are	they're

C **And what about Dave's friends? Circle the right word.**
Und was ist mit Daves Freunden? Umkringeln Sie das richtige Wort.

Example:
⟶ CoolCoCo *(ist)* | eats | (is) a rap singer too.

1 Paul *(mag)* | likes | lies | Eminem songs.

2 Joe and Emma *(sind)* | ask | are | metal fans.

3 Alicia often *(schaut)* | watches | washes | music videos.

4 Sabrina and her friend *(lieben)* | live | love | dancing.

5 Asif has got an office job too. He usually *(arbeitet)* | wears | works | a lot.

Grammar: Was jemand regelmäßig tut ⟶ G1

I read	**I often listen to music.**
you read	Ich höre oft Musik.
he/she/it reads	**Sue usually surfs the internet.**
	Sue surft meistens im Internet.
we read	
you read	**My friends watch TV all the time.**
they read	Meine Freunde sehen die ganze Zeit fern.

The test

Ewa is a hairdresser. She has got a new job at *Hannah's Hair*.
It's her first day today. She looks at the rules.

Rules at *Hannah's Hair*:

Always be polite to our customers!

– Help them with their coats.

– Ask them if they would like a cup of tea or coffee.

– Never talk about other customers.

– No mobile phones!

– No MP3 players!

hairdresser Friseur/in	
rule Regel, Vorschrift	
customer Kunde/Kundin	
coat Mantel, Jacke	
they would like sie hätten gern	
to curl kräuseln, aufdrehen	
to dry trocknen	
earphones Ohrhörer	
to answer the phone ans Telefon gehen	
Well done! Gut gemacht!	
to pass bestehen	
headphones Kopfhörer	
ringtone Klingelton	
to receive erhalten	
text SMS	
to text eine SMS-Nachricht verschicken, „simsen"	

Here's Ewa's first customer.

Ewa Good morning, Ms Hill. Can I take your coat? … Thank you. Please sit down.

Ms Hill Thank you. Can you curl my hair, please?

Ewa Of course, Ms Hill. Would you like a cup of tea or coffee?

Ms Hill No, thank you. Are you new here?

Ewa Yes, I am. My name is Ewa. I live in Park Street.

Ms Hill Park Street? Now, you must know that terrible Mrs Jackson. She lives in Park Street too.

Ewa Yes, I know Mrs Jackson. She's really … er … Your hair is now ready to dry.

Ms Hill Good. You can listen to your MP3 player then.

Ewa Oh no, I can't.

Ms Hill Why not? I can see the earphones in your pocket.

Ewa It's one of the rules here: "No MP3 players."

At this moment, Ewa's mobile phone rings.

Ms Hill You can answer your phone first.

Ewa I can't. It's the rule.

Ms Hill You're a good hairdresser, Ewa. And you know the rules. Now answer the phone. It's my daughter.

Ewa Your daughter?

Ms Hill Yes, my daughter – Hannah Hill, your new boss. Well done, Ewa! You've passed our test.

Vocabulary: Handys und Co.

– earphones, headphones, MP3 player, mobile (phone), smartphone, ringtone
– to answer the phone, to call somebody, to send a text, to receive a text, to text

Skills Tip

Lesen Sie zuerst die Arbeitsanweisung. Was **genau** müssen Sie tun?

A **Finish the sentences. Tick A or B for sentences 1–3.**
Vervollständigen Sie die Sätze. Machen Sie bei den Sätzen 1–3 ein Häkchen bei A oder B.

Skills Tip

Lesen Sie jeden Satz in Ruhe durch. Suchen Sie im Text links nach Wörtern, die auch in der Aufgabe auftauchen. Das kann Ihnen bei der Antwort helfen.

1 Ewa can't use her

A ☐ coat.

B ☐ MP3 player.

2 Ewa's first customer is

A ☐ Ms Hill.

B ☐ Hannah.

3 Ewa's customer wants

A ☐ coffee.

B ☐ nothing.

B **Match the English sentences 1–5 to the German sentences A–E. Draw lines.**
Ordnen Sie die englischen Sätze 1–5 den deutschen Sätzen A–E zu. Ziehen Sie Linien.

1 Can I take your coat?	A Natürlich.
2 Please sit down.	B Bitte nehmen Sie Platz.
3 Of course.	C Gut gemacht!
4 Would you like a cup of tea?	D Hätten Sie gern eine Tasse Tee?
5 Well done!	E Darf ich Ihnen den Mantel abnehmen?

Grammar: have got   ⟶ **G7**

I have got	I've got
you have got	you've got
he/she/it has got	he's/she's/it's got
we have got	we've got
you have got	you've got
they have got	they've got

I've got a new coat.
Ich habe einen neuen Mantel.

Mike has got two cats.
Mike hat zwei Katzen.

My parents have got a new car.
Meine Eltern haben ein neues Auto.

C **Put in 've (3x), have (1x) or has (1x). The Grammar box above can help you.**
Setzen Sie 've (3x), have (1x) oder has (1x) ein. Der Grammatik-Kasten oben kann Ihnen helfen.

1 Ewa _____ got an MP3 player and a mobile.

2 A lot of Ewa's friends _____ got smartphones.

3 Ewa texts her friends. "I _____ got a new job," she writes. "Let's go out!"

4 "Sorry. We _____ got no money," her friends write back.

5 "But you _____ got lots of time," Ewa writes. "Let's meet in the park."

Ziel: Ich kann eine förmliche Email schreiben.

A **Read the text. You do not have to understand every word.**
Lesen Sie den Text. Sie müssen nicht jedes Wort verstehen.

Rules for formal emails

1. Start with a polite phrase like "Dear Mrs Taylor".
2. Write in a clear style.
3. Keep it short.
4. No jokes and "emoticons".
5. Finish with a polite phrase like "Yours sincerely".
6. Give your full name.

Now look at the list of topics. Tick the 6 topics that are mentioned in the rules.
Nun schauen Sie sich die Liste der Themen an. Machen Sie ein Häkchen bei den 6 Themen, die in den Regeln erwähnt werden.

☐ höfliche Anrede   ☐ nie löschen   ☐ höflicher Gruß
☐ richtiges Datum   ☐ Vor-/Nachname angeben   ☐ keine Witze/„Emoticons"
☐ Text kurz halten   ☐ klarer Schreibstil   ☐ Kopie anfertigen

B **Read Sammy's email. Why is his boss angry with him?**
Lesen Sie Sammys Email. Warum ist seine Chefin wütend auf ihn?

It's Sammy's first week at work. Today he has to write an email to a music company.
This is what he writes:

To:	akhan@newmusic.co…uk	✖
Subject:	Music	

Hi
Our company makes really good shoes. We want to show them on youTube.
My boss thinks that youTube is great. I think youTube is really cool too.
I often watch the videos, usually with my friends Sally and Joe.
My boss says that our company needs some really good music for the video.
We hope that you can help us. Or are you too busy? ;-))

Bye
Sammy

phrase
Redewendung,
Ausdruck

clear
klar, deutlich

joke
Witz

Yours sincerely
Mit freundlichen
Grüßen

company
Firma

subject
Betreff

1 **Mark at least 4 things that are wrong with Sammy's email.**
Markieren Sie mindestens 4 Dinge, die in Sammys Email falsch sind.
Tipp: Sehen Sie sich die „Regeln für förmliche Emails" oben noch einmal an.

2 **Write a new email for Sammy.**
Schreiben Sie eine neue Email für Sammy.

Ziel: Ich kann ein Internet-Formular ausfüllen.

C **Your hobby is hip-hop dancing. You want to order an old DVD from a British internet shop.**
Ihr Hobby ist Hip-Hop Tanz. Sie wollen eine alte DVD bei einem britischen Internet-Shop bestellen.

1 **Read the form. Fill it out with your personal details.**
Lesen Sie das Formular. Füllen Sie es mit Ihren persönlichen Angaben aus.

2 **Note the German words for the field names on the right.**
Notieren Sie rechts die deutschen Begriffe für die Feldnamen.

New customers: Register with brit-film.com first.

Title*	○ Mr ○ Ms ○ Mrs
First name*	
Last name*	
Email address*	
Address*	
City*	
Postcode*	
Country*	
Phone number	
Date of birth	DD MM YYYY

*required fields

Feldnamen

Vorname
_____
_____
_____
_____
_____
_____
_____
_____

Grammar: There is / There are   → G7

There is / There's ...	Es ist ... / Da ist ... / Es gibt ...	**There's** a great new video.
There are ...	Es sind ... / Da sind ... / Es gibt ...	Es gibt ein tolles neues Video.
		There are lots of people in the club.
		Es sind viele Menschen im Club.

D **Tell your friends about the DVD shop. Put in *There's* or *There are*.**
The Grammar box above can help you.
Erzählen Sie Ihren Freunden von dem DVD-Shop. Setzen Sie *There's* oder *There are* ein.
Der Grammatik-Kasten oben kann Ihnen helfen.

1 *(Es gibt)* _____ a great DVD shop online.

2 *(Da sind)* _____ so many DVDs that I find interesting.

3 *(Es gibt)* _____ lots of internet shops but the others aren't very good.

4 *(Da ist)* _____ one shop that sells only hip-hop clothes.

to register (with)
sich anmelden (bei)

title
Anrede

required
erforderlich

field
Feld

clothes
Kleidung

2 In touch

Ziel: Ich kann fragen, was gewöhnlich der Fall ist. *Beispiel: Do you listen to music?*

Yasmin's questions and Hamit's answers
Yasmins Fragen und Hamits Antworten

Yasmin is a reporter. She often writes to famous people and asks them questions.
Today it's football star Hamit.

Yasmin's questions   **Hamit's answers**

Yasmin

Hamit

1. Do you use social networks?
> Yes, I do. I've got millions of friends!

2. Do you write lots of emails?
> No, I don't. I haven't got the time.

3. Does your mobile often ring?
> Yes, it does. It's terrible.

4. Does your girlfriend send you lots of emails?
> No, she doesn't. She rings me!

A What do you think? Does Hamit really know millions of people?
Was glauben Sie? Kennt Hamit wirklich Millionen Menschen?

☐ Yes, he does.
☐ No, he doesn't.

Vocabulary: Kommunikation im Netz

to blog, to chat, community, to download, email / mail, online, to post, profile, (web)site, to skype, social network

B What about you?
Und Sie?

1 Do you use social networks?
Benutzen Sie soziale Netzwerke?

☐ Yes, I do.   ☐ No, I don't.

2 Does your mobile often ring?
Klingelt Ihr Handy oft?

☐ Yes, it does.   ☐ No, it doesn't.

Grammar: Etwas <u>nicht</u> tun → G1

I don't work
you don't work
he/she/it doesn't work
we don't work
you don't work
they don't work

in touch
in Verbindung

social network
soziales Netzwerk

community
Gemeinschaft

to post something
etwas ins Internet stellen

profile
Profil, Selbstdarstellung

Terrible Tom

A **Listen to the story. Tick the right picture (1 or 2).**

A 2.2 Hören Sie sich die Geschichte an. Machen Sie ein Häkchen an das passende Bild (1 oder 2).

B **Listen to the story again. Tick A or B for sentences 1–4.**

Hören Sie sich die Geschichte noch einmal an. Machen Sie bei den Sätzen 1–4 ein Häkchen bei A oder B.

1 A ☐ Patty is Tom's teacher.
   B ☐ Patty is Tom's colleague.

2 A ☐ Melinda is a customer.
   B ☐ It's Melinda's birthday.

3 A ☐ The colleagues meet in the canteen.
   B ☐ The colleagues go home.

4 A ☐ Tom sells cars.
   B ☐ Tom is a hairdresser.

Grammar: Fragen, was gewöhnlich der Fall ist ⟶ **G1**

Do I work?	**Do you** sometimes **read** my blog?
Do you work?	Liest du manchmal mein Blog?
Does he/she/it work?	
Do we work?	**Does Mel** often **surf** the internet?
Do you work?	Surft Mel oft im Internet?
Do they work?	**Do your friends like** texting?
	Schicken deine Freunde gern SMS?

Vocabulary:
Freunde und Bekannte

– friend, boyfriend,
  girlfriend,
  partner
– neighbour, classmate
– colleague, customer,
  boss

C **Who is Jens? Fill in the right word.**

Wer ist Jens? Tragen Sie das richtige Wort ein.
Tipp: Die Antwort hinter dem Satz kann Ihnen helfen.

Example: _____ [**Do** / **Does**] Jens know Tom? – Yes, he does.

   ⟶ *Does Jens know Tom? – Yes, he does.*

1 _____ [**Do** / **Does**] Jens work at Barker's Garage too? – No, he doesn't.

2 _____ [**Do** / **Does**] Jens and Tom live in the same house? – No, they don't.

3 _____ [**Do** / **Does**] Tom and Jens often go out together? – No, they don't.

4 _____ [**Do** / **Does**] Tom call Jens his friend? – Yes, he does. Jens is one of his

social network friends!

colleague
Kollege/Kollegin

canteen
Kantine

**boyfriend/
girlfriend**
(feste/r) Freund/in

neighbour
Nachbar/in

classmate
Klassen-
kamerad/in

13

FamousMeBook

Here's an internet ad.

FamousMeBook

- Do you always stay in touch with old friends?

- Do you want to make lots of new friends?

- Do you want to share your feelings and your photos with everybody?

Come to FamousMeBook today. We offer you **VIP membership** of the world's coolest online community – FamousMeBook.

Register today and meet Very Interesting People! →

Julia likes the FamousMeBook ad. She's skyping her friend Ronnie in England.

Julia	Hi Ronnie.
Ronnie	Hi Julia. Are you back in Germany now?
Julia	Yes, I am, unfortunately. Listen, Ronnie, do you know FamousMeBook?
Ronnie	Yes, I do! Unfortunately!
Julia	What do you mean?
Ronnie	Do you remember that job interview next week that I told you about?
Julia	Yes, I do.
Ronnie	Well, I don't think that it's a good idea now.
Julia	Are you crazy? You said that Dupont's is the classiest restaurant in town.
Ronnie	Yeah, and the classiest people in town go there. <u>Real</u> VIPs, do you understand? **V**ery **I**mportant **P**eople, not **V**ery **I**diotic **P**eople, like people who use FamousMeBook!
Julia	Stop, stop, stop! What's the problem?
Ronnie	OK. Do you remember Saturday?
Julia	Do you mean Jill's party? Of course I do. It was fun. Everybody drank too much.
Ronnie	Yes, everybody. Me too. And then I put a CD in the oven.
Julia	Yes, there was smoke everywhere! I took a photo of you with your mobile.

Ronnie	Yeah, thanks for that. And when I came home late at night, I posted that photo on FamousMeBook. All my "friends" thought it was very funny. But one of my "friends" is Monsieur Dupont, unfortunately. He sent me an email. He said that in his restaurant they put food in ovens, not CDs.
Julia	Oh dear!
Ronnie	Do you understand now that I don't think it's a good idea to go there next week?

ad
Anzeige

to make friends
Freundschaften schließen

to share
teilen

feeling
Gefühl

membership
Mitgliedschaft

unfortunately
leider

job interview
Vorstellungs-gespräch

crazy
verrückt

classy
edel, elegant

real
echt, wirklich

idiotic
idiotisch

Me too.
Ich auch.

oven
Backofen

to take a photo
ein Foto machen

Vocabulary: denken, fühlen usw.

feel, know, like, love, mean, remember, think, understand, want

A **Are these statements true or false? Write your answer after the statement.**
Sind diese Aussagen richtig oder falsch? Schreiben Sie Ihre Antwort hinter die Aussage.

Skills Tip

Lesen Sie sich jede Aussage gut durch. Überlegen Sie, ob die Aussage richtig oder
falsch ist. Bilden Sie die Sätze mit „stimmt" (= richtig) oder „stimmt nicht" (= falsch),
z. B.: „Es stimmt nicht, dass die Internet-Anzeige für einen Online-Shop wirbt".

Aussage	richtig oder falsch?
1 Die Internet-Anzeige wirbt für einen Online-Shop.	falsch
2 Ronnie soll zu einem Vorstellungsgespräch kommen.	_____
3 Julia war am Samstag auch auf Jills Party.	_____
4 Ronnie legte zwei CDs in den Backofen.	_____
5 Ronnie löschte das Foto von der Party.	_____

B **Find the right word for definitions 1–4.**
Finden Sie zu den Worterklärungen 1–4 das passende Wort.

Skills Tip

Die gesuchten Wörter kommen alle im Text links vor. Wenn Sie unsicher sind, schauen Sie
dort noch einmal nach. Manchmal hilft es, wenn man ein Wort im Zusammenhang sieht.

community • food • restaurant • ~~feeling~~

1 Something that you feel: feeling _____

2 A group of people (on the internet): _____

3 A place where you can buy

and eat a meal: _____

4 What you eat: _____

C **Circle the right phrase.**
Umkringeln Sie den richtigen Ausdruck.

Example:
→ *My friend Tina* ⟨*hasn't got*⟩ *haven't got* *a social
network profile.*

1 She ⟨don't⟩ ⟨doesn't⟩ like social networks.

2 I ⟨hasn't got⟩ ⟨haven't got⟩ any problems with them.

3 What ⟨do⟩ ⟨does⟩ you think about social networks?

4 ⟨Have you got⟩ ⟨Has you got⟩ hundreds of friends too?

Grammar: Fragen, was jemand hat / → **G7**
Sagen, was jemand nicht hat

Have I got …?	I haven't got …
Have you got …?	You haven't got …
Has he/she/it got …?	He/she/it **hasn't** got …
Have we got …?	We haven't got …
Have you got …?	You haven't got …
Have they got …?	They haven't got …

Ziel: Ich kann mich vorstellen.

New at work

Alex has got a new job. In his lunch break he sees a nice young woman in the canteen.

Alex	Hi. Do you mind if I sit here?
Vanessa	No, I don't.
Alex	Thanks. My name is Alex.
Vanessa	And I'm Vanessa. Nice to meet you, Alex. Are you new here?
Alex	Yes, I am. I work in Production. I'm a machine operator. And what's your job?
Vanessa	I'm a management assistant.
Alex	And do you like it here?
Vanessa	Yes, I do. My boss is usually friendly and the pay isn't bad. And you?
Alex	Well, I like the canteen!
Vanessa	Yes, it's OK. So see you for lunch tomorrow again?
Alex	Great idea. See you for lunch tomorrow.

A   **Match questions 1 – 6 with answers A – F. Draw lines.**
Ordnen Sie die Fragen 1 – 6 den Antworten A – F zu. Ziehen Sie Linien.

1 Do you mind if I sit here?	A Yes, I am.
2 What's your name?	B I'm a machine operator.
3 Are you new here?	C No, I don't.
4 Where do you work?	D My name is Alex.
5 What's your job?	E Yes, I do.
6 Do you like it here?	F I work in Production.

lunch break
Mittagspause

to mind
etwas dagegen haben

production
Produktion

machine operator
Maschinen-führer/in

management assistant
Bürokauffrau/-mann

pay
Bezahlung, Gehalt

firm
Firma

B   **Complete Alex' email to his friend. If you need help, read the dialogue above again.**
Vervollständigen Sie Alex' Email an seinen Freund. Wenn Sie Hilfe brauchen, lesen Sie den Dialog oben noch einmal.

I talked to one of my new colleagues today. Her name is _____ [1] and she's

really nice. She works as a _____ [2] in my new

firm. Vanessa likes the firm. She says her _____ [3] is usually friendly

and she thinks the pay is OK. She wants to see me again for _____ [4]

tomorrow – isn't that great?!

Ziel: Ich kann für ein soziales Netzwerk ein Profil von mir anfertigen.

C **Read the three profiles. Then read the information 1–3 below.**
Put the right name under each profile.
Lesen Sie die drei Profile. Dann lesen Sie die Informationen 1–3 darunter.
Schreiben Sie den richtigen Namen unter jedes Profil.

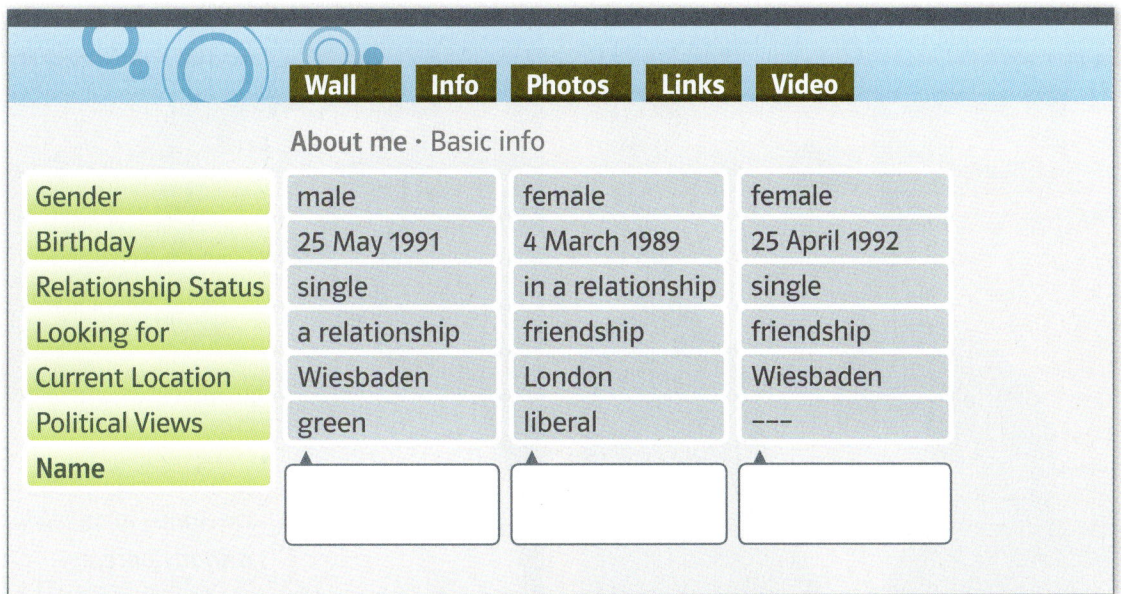

	Wall	Info	Photos	Links	Video

About me · Basic info

Gender	male	female	female
Birthday	25 May 1991	4 March 1989	25 April 1992
Relationship Status	single	in a relationship	single
Looking for	a relationship	friendship	friendship
Current Location	Wiesbaden	London	Wiesbaden
Political Views	green	liberal	---
Name			

1 Jessica has got a boyfriend. She's looking for friendship. She doesn't live in Wiesbaden.

2 Tarek is looking for a relationship. His birthday is on the 25th. His political views are green.

3 Anna is single. She lives in Wiesbaden. She doesn't tell us her political views.

Grammar: mein, dein, usw.   → **G 13**

my	**Die Formen bleiben immer gleich:**
your	
his/her/its	That's **her** profile. Das ist ihr Profil.
our	I don't like **her** music. Mir gefällt ihre Musik nicht.
your	
their	Tim and Tom are **her** brothers. Tim und Tom sind ihre Brüder.

D **Fill in the correct English words. Tip: They are all in the Grammar Box above.**
Tragen Sie die richtigen englischen Wörter ein. Tipp: Die Wörter stehen alle im
Grammatik-Kasten oben.

1 Mark is my boyfriend. _____ [**seine**] favourite music is techno.

2 We often go to clubs together. We meet _____ [**unsere**] friends there.

3 My father thinks that's OK. He says, "It's _____ [**dein**] life now.
You can do what you like."

4 Lots of my friends have got more problems at home. _____ [**ihre**]
parents are more difficult.

wall
(Pinn-)Wand

basic info
allgemeine
Informationen

gender
Geschlecht

male/female
männlich/weiblich

relationship
Beziehung

status
Status

looking for
auf der Suche
nach

friendship
Freundschaft

current location
derzeitiger
Wohnort

political views
politische
Einstellung

3 A place of my own

Ziel: Ich kann sagen, was ich gerade mache. *Beispiel: I'm reading.*

I'm Anna. I've got a place of my own.

I'm Sam. I'm still living with my parents.

What are Anna and Sam doing at the moment? Look at the photos and read the sentences.
Was machen Anna und Sam im Moment? Schauen Sie sich die Fotos an und lesen Sie die Sätze.

I'm cleaning my kitchen at the moment.

Now I'm doing my washing.

I'm phoning my friend.

Right now, I'm waiting for my meal.

a place of my own	meine eigene Bleibe
still	immer noch
to do the washing	die Wäsche machen
right now	im Augenblick
meal	Essen, Mahlzeit

1 Who's talking here?
Wer spricht hier?

A ☐ Anna   **B** ☐ Sam

2 And who's talking here?
Und wer spricht hier?

A ☐ Anna   **B** ☐ Sam

The pizza problem

A **Listen first. Then tick the right picture (1–3).**

A2.3 Hören Sie zuerst zu. Machen Sie dann ein Häkchen an das passende Bild (1–3).

 **1**

 **2**

 **3**

B **Listen again. Tick A or B for sentences 1–4.**
Hören Sie noch einmal zu. Machen Sie bei den Sätzen 1–4 ein Häkchen
bei A oder B.

1 **Tina is making**

A ☐ breakfast.

B ☐ a salad.

2 **Paul is doing**

A ☐ the lasagne.

B ☐ the pizzas.

3 **The pizzas have to go in the oven for**

A ☐ eleven minutes.

B ☐ seven minutes.

4 **Tina is checking**

A ☐ Paul.

B ☐ the packet.

C **And Tina's neighbours? Put in *is* or *are*.**
Und Tinas Nachbarn? Fügen Sie *is* oder *are* ein.

Example: Ms Fox _____ cutting some carrots.
→ *Ms Fox is cutting some carrots.*

1 Her partner _____ making tea.

2 Ben _____ taking some cookies out
of the oven.

3 Lisa _____ washing the dishes.

4 May and Lee _____ eating.

Grammar: Die -ing-Form → **G 2**

Verb	+	-ing
cook	→	cook**ing**
cut	→	cut**t**ing
make	→	mak**ing**

Vocabulary: Was man im Alltag tut

clean, cook, do the washing, iron,
listen to music, make the bed, play games,
phone friends, read, surf the internet,
wash the dishes, watch TV

Grammar: Was jemand gerade tut → **G 2**

Right now, I'm reading.
Im Augenblick lese ich.

Dan is watching TV at the moment.
Dan sieht gerade fern.

We're just doing our homework.
Wir machen soeben unsere Hausaufgaben.

My parents are cooking now.
Meine Eltern kochen jetzt.

Are you listening to me?
Hörst du mir zu?

---

salad
Salat

carrot
Möhre, Karotte

just
gerade, soeben

to iron
bügeln

**to wash the
dishes**
abwaschen,
spülen

A place of our own

⊙ A2.4 Tracy and Denzil are looking for a flat. They are reading this advert:

Modern flat, kitchen, living room, bathroom, bedroom. Cable TV. Broadband internet.
Tables, bed, chairs, sofa, shelves – everything!
Only £500 per month.
→ Phone 543769, "Matt's Flats", Mr Shrekly

Do you think Tracy and Denzil find the flat interesting? Read more.
Denken Sie, dass Tracy und Denzil die Wohnung interessant finden? Lesen Sie weiter.

It's Saturday. Tracy and Denzil are driving to see the flat. They're in Tracy's car.

Denzil	I hope it's a nice flat.
Tracy	Well, I'm sure it's better than the old flat last week.
Denzil	Yes, we want a modern flat with modern furniture.
Tracy	And the most important thing: we want a place of our own!

Denzil	Exactly. Your parents are OK, but, er, …
Tracy	… they're my parents!
Denzil	Yes, and our room there is big enough, but …
Tracy	… it's in their house! Look, Denzil, I want to move out too. We don't have to discuss it again. We aren't staying at my parents' house!
Denzil	Look, we're here. I like the colour of the building. Very nice!

15 minutes later …

Denzil	Let's drive away – fast!
Tracy	Yes. I'm still shaking. That terrible furniture! And the awful smell. Uggh!
Denzil	I'm sure there are rats in the building. This must be the worst flat in England.
Tracy	Forget Mr Shrekly's flat. We aren't moving out! We're staying at my parents' house.

flat
Wohnung

advert
Anzeige

cable TV
Kabelfernsehen

broadband
Breitband

shelf, shelves
Regal, Regale

Exactly.
Genau.

enough
genug

to discuss
diskutieren

to shake
zittern

furniture
Möbel

awful
furchtbar

smell
Geruch

rat
Ratte

the worst flat
die schlimmste Wohnung

to move out
ausziehen

Vocabulary: In der Wohnung (Nomen)

– bathroom, bedroom, kitchen, living room
– bed, chair, shelf, sofa, table
– cable TV, broadband

A Questions on the text. Answer the questions.
Fragen zum Text. Beantworten Sie die Fragen.

> **Skills Tip**
>
> Meistens sind die Fragen in der Reihenfolge des Textes aufgeschrieben, das heißt die Antwort auf die erste Frage findet sich eher oben im Text, die Antwort auf die letzte Frage eher unten usw.

1 How much does the flat cost per month? £_____

2 How are Tracy and Denzil getting to the flat? They're _____

3 Who likes the colour of the building? _____

4 Where do Tracy and Denzil want to stay now? At Tracy's _____

B Who is talking? Choose the right name(s) for sentences 1–3.
Wer spricht? Wählen Sie den/die richtigen Namen für die Sätze 1–3.

Mr Shrekly • Tracy and Denzil • Tracy's parents

1 "Of course it's no problem that they're still living with us." _____

2 "We aren't looking for a flat any more." _____

3 "I can't understand why they're all running away …" _____

C **1** Match the sentence parts. Draw lines.
Ordnen Sie die Satzhälften einander zu. Ziehen Sie Linien.

1 The name of the building is …	○	○	A awful!
2 Denzil: Mr Shrekly's flat …	○	○	B big enough for them all.
3 Tracy: The smell of the flat was …	○	○	C not "Matt's Rats"!
4 Her parents' house is …	○	○	D is the worst flat in England!

2 Look at the Grammar box. Then translate the phrases 1–3 into English.
Schauen Sie sich den Grammatik-Kasten an. Dann übersetzen Sie die Wendungen 1–3 ins Englische.

Grammar: Wessen?		⟶ G 14
Tracy's car	**my parents' house**	**the colour of the building**
Tracys Auto	das Haus meiner Eltern	die Farbe des Gebäudes
(= eine Person)	(= mehrere Personen)	(= Sachen)

1 Sams Haus	2 die Wohnung meiner Freunde	3 die Farbe des Autos
_____	_____	_____

Ziel: Ich kann in einem Geschäft als Kunde/Kundin oder Verkäufer/in ein Gespräch führen.

Getting started

Sarah Brown from England has found a job in Germany. She is just moving into a place of her own. She wants to paint her flat, so she is going to a big shop.

Assistant	Kann ich Ihnen behilflich sein?
Sarah	Guten Abend. Ich … Sorry, I don't speak German very well. Do you speak English?
Assistant	Yes, I do. How can I help you?
Sarah	I'm just moving into a new flat. I'm looking for paint and paintbrushes.
Assistant	They're over here. All the different colours and sizes. What colour are you looking for?
Sarah	Yellow.
Assistant	Here you are. Anything else?
Sarah	No, that's it. Thank you for your help. Bye.
Assistant	Thank you. Goodbye.

A **Another conversation.**
Ein anderes Gespräch.

1 **Look at the sentences 1–7. Who is speaking?**
Write A for the shop assistant or C for the customer.
Sehen Sie sich die Sätze 1–7 an. Wer spricht? Schreiben Sie A für den Verkäufer / die Verkäuferin oder C für den Kunden / die Kundin.

1 ☐ Of course. Here you are. Anything else?

2 ☐ How can I help you?

3 ☐ No, that's it. Bye.

4 ☐ I'm looking for nail polish.

5 ☐ Goodbye.

6 ☐ Black, of course.

7 ☐ Nail polish is over here. What colour are you looking for?

2 **Act out the dialogue.**
Spielen Sie das Gespräch nach.

B **Finish Sarah's email. Put the verbs in brackets into the -ing form.**
Vervollständigen Sie Sarahs Email. Bringen Sie die Verben in Klammern in die -ing-Form.

> ✖
>
> Hi Robin
>
> Thanks for your mail. **You're** busy? Not as busy as I am! I'm sure you aren't
>
> [1 paint] _____ a new flat at the moment. And you aren't
>
> [2 repair] _____ windows. Are you [3 learn] _____
>
> German too? And are you [4 start] _____ a new job? See?!
>
> I must be the busiest girl in Germany. But I love it!
>
> Love, Sarah

to paint; paint
malen, anstreichen; Farbe

(shop) assistant
Verkäufer/in

paintbrush
Farbpinsel

over here/there
hier/dort

size
Größe

Here you are.
Hier, bitte.

Anything else?
Noch etwas?

nail polish
Nagellack

Ziel: Ich kann beim Einkaufen Dinge miteinander vergleichen.

In a flower shop

Paula works in a flower shop. Today her customer is Vitali. He's looking for something unusual.

Paula Guten Tag. Sie wünschen?

Vitali Guten Tag. Eh, do you speak English?

Paula Well, I can try. What would you like?

Vitali I'm looking for a nice plant for my new flat. I'd like something unusual.

Paula OK. Here you are. This is the most unusual plant in the shop.

Vitali That looks fine, but it's too big. It should be smaller than that.

Paula How about this one? But it isn't as unusual as the other plant.

Vitali That's fine. How much does it cost?

Paula It's twelve euros.

Vitali That's more expensive than I thought.

Paula Well, it's the cheapest plant that we've got.

Vitali OK, I'll take it. Thank you very much.

> **Vocabulary: Wie etwas ist (Adjektive)**
>
> beautiful, busy, dangerous, difficult, dirty, easy, great, famous, fantastic, terrible, unfriendly

---

A **Look at the photos. Tick A or B for sentences 1–3.**
Sehen Sie sich die Fotos an. Machen Sie bei den Sätzen 1–3 ein Häkchen bei A oder B.

1 The brown dog is

A ☐ bigger

B ☐ smaller

than the black dog.

2 The glass on the right is

A ☐ the smallest

B ☐ the fullest

glass.

3 The girl on the left looks as

A ☐ friendly

B ☐ unfriendly

as the girl on the right.

B **Match the beginnings (1–4) to the endings (A–D).**
Ordnen Sie die Satzanfänge (1–4) den Satzenden (A–D) zu.

☐ 1 Good morning. I'm looking for …

☐ 2 What would …

☐ 3 It's nice, but it's …

☐ 4 That's fine. How much …

A … more expensive than I thought.

B … an interesting souvenir.

C … does it cost?

D … you like?

> **Grammar: Vergleiche**   → **G 11**
>
> | smaller (than …) | the cheapest | as unusual as … |
> |---|---|---|
> | kleiner (als …) | der/die/das billigste | so ungewöhnlich wie … |
> | more expensive (than …) | the most unusual | |
> | teurer (als …) | der/die/das ungewöhnlichste | |

unusual
ungewöhnlich

What would you like?
Was wünschen Sie?

plant
Pflanze

I'd like …
Ich hätte gern …

on the left
links

4 On the move

Ziel: Ich kann sagen, was in der Vergangenheit geschah. *Beispiel: Yesterday I watched TV.*

What did these people do last summer? First look at the photos.
Was haben diese Menschen letzten Sommer gemacht? Sehen Sie sich zuerst die Fotos an.

Liv, Mark, Anna and Pedro

Hassan

Marisa

A Who said what? Read the statements and tick the right number.
Wer sagte was? Lesen Sie die Aussagen und machen Sie ein Häkchen an die passende Zahl.

☐ ☐ ☐ Last summer I took driving lessons.
1 2 3

☐ ☐ ☐ Last summer we flew to Spain and rented a car there.
1 2 3

☐ ☐ ☐ Last summer I bought an old car and repaired it.
1 2 3

Vocabulary: Fortbewegung
– to drive, to fly, to ride, to walk
– bike, bus, camper van, car, jeep, lorry, motorbike, plane, train, truck, van

B And you (or your friends)?
Und Sie (oder Ihre Freunde)?

Last summer _____ stayed at home in the holidays.

Last year _____ took driving lessons.

_____

---

on the move
in Bewegung

driving lessons
Fahrstunden

we flew
wir flogen
(Grundform:
to fly)

Spain
Spanien

to rent
mieten

camper van
Wohnmobil

lorry, truck
LKW

motorbike
Motorrad

van
(Klein-)
Transporter

Rent-a-Wreck

A **Listen to Sue's story. Tick the right picture (1–3).**

A2.5 Hören Sie sich Sues Geschichte an. Machen Sie ein Häkchen an das passende Bild (1–3).

1

2

3

B **Listen to the story again. Tick *true* or *false* for sentences 1–4.**

Hören Sie sich die Geschichte noch einmal an. Machen Sie bei den Sätzen 1–4 ein Häkchen bei *richtig* oder *falsch*.

	true	false
1 Sue's brother Tim came to the airport.	☐	☐
2 Sue rented an expensive camper van at the airport.	☐	☐
3 Sue bought an old car in Denver.	☐	☐
4 Sue visited her brother Tim in hospital.	☐	☐

Grammar: Was in der Vergangenheit geschah → **G 3**

– regelmäßig: Verb + **-ed**
– unregelmäßig: besondere Formen
   → vordere Umschlagseite (innen)

Last week I walk**ed** to town.
Letzte Woche ging ich zu Fuß in die Stadt.

Pat **drove** to London **yesterday**.
Pat fuhr gestern nach London.

C **Summer holidays. Fill in the correct word.**

Sommerferien. Fügen Sie das richtige Wort ein.

Example: → *Last year we stayed [stayed/stood] at home in our holidays.*

1 But the weather was awful last summer – it

_____ [**rained/ran**] all the time!

2 My friend Alina _____ [**said/told**]

me about a good website last month.

3 So last weekend I _____

[**liked/looked**] at holidays in Spain on the internet.

4 And yesterday I _____

[**booked/rented**] a holiday in Alicante!

Grammar: → **G 3**
Vergangenheit – regelmäßige Verben

Verb + **-ed**
walk → walk**ed**
cycle → cycl**ed**
try → tr**ied**
stop → stop**ped**

wreck
Wrack

to cycle
Rad fahren

My first car

Sharon had her driving test last week. Did she pass it? What do you think?
Find out if you were right.

 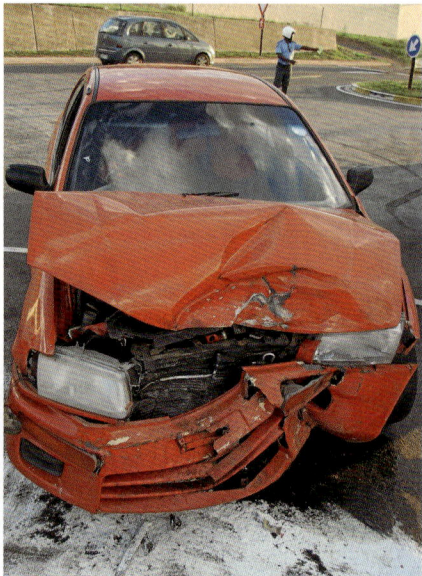

Uncle Bob	Hello, Sharon. So you passed your driving test? Well done!
Sharon	Thanks, Uncle Bob. It was easier than I thought. Now I need a car.
Uncle Bob	Ah, yes. I remember my first car. It was a used car of course, but modern for the time. It had a CD player, not a cassette player! We all thought that cassette players were – what do you young people say – "they were *so* old technology"! Of course there weren't any MP3 players or satnavs yet.
Sharon	Oh, I see.
Uncle Bob	And my first trip in my new car – well, I was a little nervous. I wanted to go to a party. My boot was full of drinks because I was the only person who had a car. I really didn't want to have an accident! But I wanted to listen to my new CD. So I looked away from the road for two seconds and put the CD into the player. Suddenly I was on the wrong side of the road and crashed my car into a phone box! My car was a wreck. Your grandad was very angry. He bought me the car, you see.
Sharon	Wow. Did grandad buy you another car?
Uncle Bob	Of course not. I had to ride my bike again!
Sharon	Poor you! Sorry, Uncle Bob, I have to go now. I'm going to Wickham – half an hour by bus.
Uncle Bob	But only ten minutes by car. You can drive my old car – with your new driving licence.
Sharon	Really? Well, thank you, Uncle Bob!
Uncle Bob	That's OK. Just put the CD in *before* you start, OK?
Sharon	CD? That's *so* old technology!

used
gebraucht

cassette
Kassette

technology
Technologie

satnav
Satelliten-
navigations-
system, „Navi"

not yet
noch nicht

boot
Kofferraum

accident
Unfall

**to crash the car
into something**
mit dem Auto
in etwas
hineinkrachen

phone box
Telefonzelle

driving licence
Führerschein

Vocabulary: Auto fahren

– to take driving lessons, to pass a driving test, to have a driving licence
– to drive a car, to ride a (motor)bike, to go by bus, to take a train
– to crash a car into something, to have an accident

A **Decide if these statements are true or false. Write your answer after the statement.**
Entscheiden Sie, ob diese Aussagen richtig oder falsch sind. Schreiben Sie Ihre Antwort hinter die Aussage.

Skills Tip

Lesen Sie sich jede Aussage gut durch. Vergleichen Sie sie mit der passenden Stelle im Text, bevor Sie entscheiden.

Statement	true or false?
1 Sharon thinks the driving test was difficult.	false
2 Uncle Bob's first car had a satnav.	
3 Uncle Bob had an accident with his first car.	
4 Uncle Bob bought Sharon a car.	
5 Sharon is going to walk to Wickham.	

B **Find the right word in the text for definitions 1–5.**
Finden Sie zu den Worterklärungen 1–5 das passende Wort im Text.

1 A man who is the brother of your father or mother: uncle

2 Something that helps drivers to find the way: _____

3 A place in a car that you use for bags, drinks, etc.: _____

4 Three words that mean 30 minutes: _____

5 Something that shows that you can drive a car: _____

Grammar: Nähere Beschreibungen   ⟿ **G10**

Sachen: **I bought the car which/that I showed you last week.**
Ich habe das Auto, das ich dir letzte Woche zeigte, gekauft.

Personen: **The woman who/that drives the blue car is my boss.**
Die Frau, die das blaue Auto fährt, ist meine Chefin.

C **Circle the right time phrase.**
Umkringeln Sie die richtige Zeitangabe.

Example: → *My colleague flew to Spain* (last month) right now .

1 I parked my car behind the garage usually | yesterday .

2 Did Marija pass her driving test last week | tomorrow ?

3 The car that I drove last year | next week didn't have a satnav.

4 The man who gave me his car at this moment | last night

is my friend Jack.

Grammar: do/does (simple present)
→ **did (simple past)**   ⟿ **G1+3**

Does Bob often watch TV?
Sieht Bob oft fern?

→ **Did** Bob watch TV last night?
Hat Bob gestern Abend ferngesehen?

Ziel: Ich kann Reisewege beschreiben.

How do I get to . . . ?

⌖ A2.6 Jan from Holland works at a building firm. Right now he's talking to Karen.

Jan	So how do I get to Westwood tomorrow?
Karen	Do you want to go by car or use public transport?
Jan	I'm not sure. I don't have to go by car. My appointment is at 9.30 a.m.
Karen	You shouldn't go by car then. Take the 8.45 train to Eastwood Station. Be careful: You mustn't take the 8.48 – it's a fast train that doesn't stop at Eastwood.
Jan	OK. Do I have to change trains?
Karen	No. The train goes right through to Eastwood. When you get off the train, you should look for a taxi.
Jan	OK, Karen. Thanks for your help.

Vocabulary: sollen – müssen – nicht dürfen

You **should** **take** the bus.
Du solltest den Bus nehmen.
I **have to** **be** home at 8 o'clock.
Ich muss um 8 Uhr zu Hause sein.
He **mustn't** **turn** right.
Er darf (!) nicht rechts abbiegen.

A **Match the English sentences 1–3 to the German sentences A–C. Draw lines.**
Ordnen Sie die englischen Sätze 1–3 den deutschen Sätzen A–C zu. Ziehen Sie Linien.

1 You should turn left there.	A Du musst dort nicht rechts abbiegen.
2 You don't have to turn right there.	B Du solltest dort links abbiegen.
3 You mustn't turn left there.	C Du darfst dort nicht links abbiegen.

B **Two days later. Read Jan's story. Then put in the right verbs.**
Zwei Tage später. Lesen Sie Jans Geschichte. Dann fügen Sie die richtigen Verben ein.
Wenn Sie Hilfe brauchen, schauen Sie noch einmal in den Text oben.

didn't go • didn't stop • got • used • went

Karen Hi Jan. How was your trip to Westwood yesterday?

Jan Expensive! I _____ [1] by car, I _____ [2] public

transport, like you said. Unfortunately, I took the wrong train. It was the 8.48 and it

_____ [3] at Eastwood, it _____ [4] right through to

Bristol. So I _____ [5] off the train there and took a taxi back to

Westwood. I arrived at 9.25 – but I had to pay a lot of money!

---

to get (to . . .)
(nach . . .)
kommen,
gelangen

building firm
Baufirma

public transport
öffentlicher
Nahverkehr

appointment
Termin,
Verabredung

mustn't
nicht dürfen

to change trains
umsteigen

right through
direkt durch

to get off
aussteigen

you should
du solltest

to turn left/right
links/rechts
abbiegen

Ziel: Ich kann Wegbeschreibungen geben.

Giving directions

. Last month Mia and Finn were on holiday in Newtown.
. They wanted to go to the department store.
. So they asked a young man: "Excuse me, could you tell
. us the way to the department store, please?"

5 "Yes, of course," he said. "Go straight ahead.
. Cross High Street. The department store is behind
. the hospital on the left."

. "No, it's not!" said a woman who stood next to them.
. "That's the tourist information! Listen. Go straight
10 ahead and turn right into High Street over there. Go
. along High Street. Cross King Street. The department
. store is on your right, opposite the church."

. A policeman came past. "Opposite the church?
. That's the pub! Now listen to me. Go straight ahead.
15 Follow Green Street until you get to Market Street.
. Turn right there. The department store is behind the
. post office."

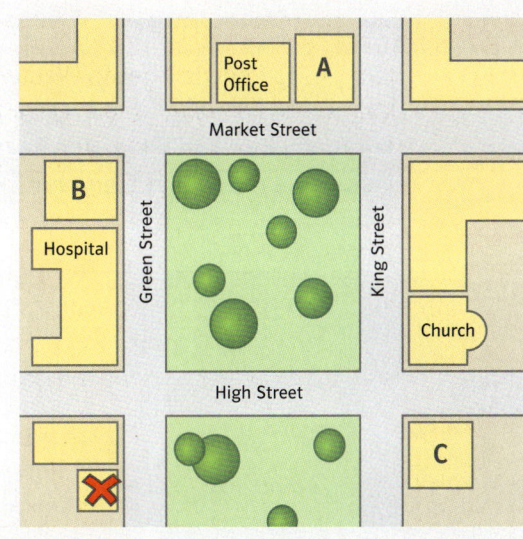

Vocabulary: Wo? Wohin?

– at, behind, between, in, in front of,
  next to, on, opposite, under
– across, along, down, from, into, off,
  over, through, to

A **Look at the map. Mia and Finn are at X. Now read the text carefully.**
What buildings are A, B and C?
Sehen Sie sich die Karte an. Mia und Finn befinden sich bei X.
Lesen Sie nun aufmerksam den Text. Was sind A, B und C für Gebäude?

A: _____   B: _____   C: _____

B **Where are they? Look at the photos. Fill in the correct words.**
Tip: Look at the Vocabulary Box above.
Wo sind sie? Schauen Sie sich die Fotos an. Tragen Sie die richtigen Wörter ein.
Tipp: Schauen Sie in den *Vocabulary*-Kasten oben.

1 The dog is _____ the sofa.
2 The girl is _____ the umbrella.
3 The child is _____ the tree.

directions	Wegbeschreibung
department store	Kaufhaus
straight ahead	geradeaus
to cross	überqueren
next to	neben
along	entlang
opposite	gegenüber (von)
church	Kirche
pub	Kneipe
between	zwischen
in front of	vor
umbrella	Regenschirm

5 You need me!

Ziel: Ich kann sagen, was ich in der Zukunft tun werde. *Beispiel: I'll work.*

What will Ben and Elena do? Read the dialogue.
Was werden Ben und Elena tun? Lesen Sie den Dialog.

Elena

Ben

> Ben, what will you do after school next year?

> I'm good at repairing things. I'll find a job as a car mechanic.

> But the firms won't take you without an apprenticeship.

> We'll see. What are your plans for the future, Elena?

> I won't start a family soon. First I'll do an apprenticeship as a hairdresser.

A **What are Ben and Elena talking about – their past, their present or their future?**
Worüber sprechen Ben und Elena – ihre Vergangenheit, ihre Gegenwart oder ihre Zukunft?

_____

Vocabulary: Fähigkeiten
I'm good at …
languages, listening, maths, organizing, talking, using a computer, working with my hands, writing

car mechanic
Auto-
mechaniker/in

apprenticeship
Lehre, Ausbildung

language
Sprache

B **What about you?**
Und Sie?

In ten years I'll _____

_____

_____

Forget the interview!

A   **Listen to the telephone dialogue. Tick the right pair of pictures (1 or 2).**

♫ A2.7   Hören Sie sich den Telefondialog an. Machen Sie ein Häkchen an das passende Bildpaar (1 oder 2).

B   **Listen to the dialogue again. Tick A or B for sentences 1–4.**

Hören Sie sich den Dialog noch einmal an. Machen Sie bei den Sätzen 1–4 ein Häkchen bei A oder B.

1   A ☐   Peter's interview is in the morning.   **3**   A ☐   Peter wants to wear a suit.

    B ☐   Peter's interview is in the afternoon.   B ☐   Peter wants to wear jeans and a T-shirt.

2   A ☐   Peter wants to come earlier.   **4**   A ☐   Jenny Williams is an assistant.

    B ☐   Peter wants to come later.   B ☐   Jenny Williams is the boss.

Grammar: Was in der Zukunft (nicht) geschehen wird   ↗ **G 5**

will (Kurzform **'ll**) + Verb	will not (Kurzform **won't**) + Verb
I'll start an apprenticeship **next year.** Nächstes Jahr werde ich eine Ausbildung anfangen.	**In the future** Sharif **won't** work at Webb's any more. In der Zukunft wird Sharif nicht mehr für Webb's arbeiten.

C   **Everything will be different in the future. Finish the sentences. Use *will/'ll* 😊 or *won't* 😦 .**

In der Zukunft wird alles anders sein. Vervollständigen Sie die Sätze.
Benutzen Sie *will/'ll* 😊 oder *won't* 😦 .

Example: → *Dana goes to school every day.* 😦 *In the future she won't go to school any more.*

1   We have to do lots of tests every month.

 😦 In the future we _____ have to do tests any more.

2   Sam often doesn't get up before 11.

 😊 In the future he _____ get up a lot earlier all the time!

3   At the moment Jenny goes out every night.

 😦 In the future she _____ go out every night any more.

4   There aren't many jobs for young people.

 😊 In the future there _____ be more jobs.

suit
Anzug; Kostüm

not . . . any more
nicht mehr

A dream job?

Tarek Miller is 18. He lives in London with his parents. Tarek is looking for a job – when he isn't too tired. On the internet he finds this job advert:

> ## Mädchen (oder Junge) für alles gesucht!
>
> German TV star in California needs a personal assistant to look after his two crazy children, cook (German food too!), drive everybody around and do many other jobs.
>
> You should like children, speak English and German, be a good cook, have a clean driving licence – and always do what I tell you!
>
> Interested? Send application by email to: ▶ hans.german@staragency…com

Tarek is interested! He writes a job application:

> . Dear Mr German
>
> . I saw your advert for a personal assistant online and I am now writing to apply for
> . the position.
>
> . I am sure that I am the right man for this job:
> 5 – I am very good at looking after crazy children because I was a crazy child myself.
> . – I didn't have German at school, but I know more than just "Bayern München" and
> . "Prost"! And I promise I will learn ten German words a day if I get the job.
> . – Cooking is no problem if you like canned soup. I am sure that I will quickly learn how
> . to cook sauerkraut for you every day.
> 10 – Chauffeur is my dream job. My driving licence will soon be clean again, and I promise
> . I won't drink alcohol any more. (Have you got a Cadillac? I love Cadillacs!)
>
> . It has always been my dream to work as a personal assistant and I've always wanted
> . to see California.
>
> . I look forward to hearing from you. Of course I would gladly come to California for an
> 15 interview. (Can I bring my mother too? I really hate flying.)
>
> . Yours sincerely
> . Tarek Miller

Vocabulary: Rund um die Bewerbung

(job) advert, apply, application, apprenticeship, (job) interview, look forward to hearing from …, position

---

personal assistant
persönliche/r Assistent/in

to look after
betreuen

application
Bewerbung

to apply (for)
sich bewerben (um)

position
(Arbeits-)Stelle

to promise
versprechen

canned soup
Suppe aus der Dose

chauffeur
Chauffeur/in, Fahrer/in

alcohol
Alkohol

to look forward to hearing from …
sich darauf freuen, von … zu hören

I would
ich würde

gladly
gern

A **Finish the sentences. Write one or two English words.**
Vervollständigen Sie die Sätze. Schreiben Sie ein oder zwei englische Wörter.

> **Skills Tip**
>
> Lesen Sie jeden Satz in der Aufgabe gründlich durch. Machen Sie sich klar, was gefragt ist.
> Suchen Sie dann nach der richtigen Stelle im Text und finden Sie die passende Ergänzung.

1 A German TV star is looking for a personal assistant for his home in _____.

2 Tarek Miller is interested in the job. He writes an _____.

3 Tarek promises that he won't drink _____ any more.

4 Tarek has a problem with planes. He doesn't like _____.

B **Give the opposite of the <u>underlined</u> words below. (You can find them all in the text.)**
Geben Sie das Gegenteil der <u>unterstrichenen</u> Wörter unten an. (Sie finden sie alle im Text.)

1 drive <u>nobody</u> around   _____

2 you should <u>hate</u> children   _____

3 be a <u>bad</u> cook   _____

4 I will <u>slowly</u> learn   _____

> **Grammar:** **Fragen, was in der Zukunft geschehen wird**   ⤳ **G 5**
>
> Satzstellung: **Will** you **miss** school *next year*?
>   **Wirst** du die Schule *nächstes Jahr* vermissen?

C **Tarek's interview. Match the questions 1–4 to the answers A–D.**
Tareks Bewerbungsgespräch. Ordnen Sie den Fragen 1–4 die Antworten A–D zu.

1 Will your German get better in the future?	A No, I didn't.
2 Did you learn German at school as a kid?	B No, I haven't.
3 Have you still got a drinking problem?	C Yes, it is.
4 Is flying usually a problem for you?	D Yes, it will.

D **Circle the right word. The Grammar Box can help you.**
Umkringeln Sie das richtige Wort. Der *Grammar*-Kasten kann Ihnen helfen.

> **Grammar:**   ⤳ **G 13**
> **Über jemanden oder etwas sprechen**
>
> | I | you | he | she | it |
> |---|---|---|---|---|
> | me | you | him | her | it |
> | we | you | they | | |
> | us | you | them | | |

1 The German star: "Tarek is interesting. I'll give [him] [them] a chance."

2 Tarek: "I'm so happy! The German star has invited [me] [you] for an interview."

3 The star's children: "Hi Tarek! We're his crazy children. Do you like [her] [us]?"

4 Tarek: "My parents are great. I'll phone [it] [them] every day from California."

The right clothes

Leyla works in a clothes shop. She loves helping customers.

Leyla	Good morning. How can I help you?
Customer	Hi. I'm looking for something special to wear. Hm, I like this short green dress! No, too short. What about this sexy pink top?
Leyla	Well, it depends. What do you need it for?
Customer	For my first job interview.
Leyla	What?! Well … I wouldn't recommend party clothes for a job interview.
Customer	But I don't want to spend money on things that I'll never wear again.
Leyla	You'll need some smart clothes in the job, too. Is it an office job?
Customer	Yes, it is.
Leyla	White blouse, blue suit. Here, I think you should try this.

A few minutes later …

Customer	Wow. You were right. It doesn't look bad at all.
Leyla	Exactly. If you get the job, you can always buy another blouse so you can change the look.
Customer	If I get the job, I'll come here again – for some party clothes!

Vocabulary:
Ratschläge erteilen

It depends.
I wouldn't recommend …
I think you should …
Why don't you …?

A   **What is the dialogue about? Read the summaries carefully and tick the right one.**
Worum geht es in dem Dialog? Lesen Sie die Zusammenfassungen sorgfältig und machen Sie ein Häkchen an die richtige Zusammenfassung.

A ☐ Junge Frau erklärt Verkäuferin, welche Kleidung für Bewerbungsgespräche geeignet ist.

B ☐ Büroangestellte sagt junger Frau, wie man an Bürojobs kommt.

C ☐ Verkäuferin hilft junger Frau, die passende Kleidung auszusuchen.

D ☐ Junge Frau kauft mithilfe der Verkäuferin tolle Partyklamotten.

Vocabulary: Kleidung

blouse, coat, dress, leather shoes, shirt, skirt, suit, tie

B   **Finish the young woman's email.**
Vervollständigen Sie die Email der jungen Frau.

Hi Linda,

Yesterday I bought some new clothes for my _____ [1]

next week. There was a very helpful _____ [2].

I'll wear a blue _____ [3] and a white _____ [4] – smart!

Love, Kirsty

special
besondere/r/s

to depend
darauf ankommen

to recommend
empfehlen

to spend
ausgeben

smart
schick

blouse
Bluse

look
Aussehen

leather
Leder

skirt
Rock

tie
Krawatte

Ziel: Ich kann ein Email-Bewerbungsschreiben formulieren.

C **Anna is looking for a job in tourism. She finds an advert on the internet. Read the advert.**
Anna sucht eine Stelle im Tourismusbereich. Im Internet findet sie eine Anzeige. Lesen Sie die Anzeige.

German/English Salesperson

Tour Tanzania are looking for German and English-speaking salespeople. Must have good computer skills, be enthusiastic and be a good team player. 23 – 35 years old.

Applications in English with attached CV (pdf) to: ▶ paul.green@tourtanzania…com

---

D **Anna applies for the job. Read her application letter. Then match paragraphs 1 – 9 of Anna's email to the parts of an application letter (A – I) below.**
Anna bewirbt sich um die Stelle. Lesen Sie ihr Bewerbungsschreiben. Dann ordnen Sie die Absätze 1 – 9 von Annas Email den Teilen eines Bewerbungsschreibens (A – I) zu.

Subject:	Job application German/English Salesperson **1**

Dear Mr Green **2**

I am writing to apply for the position of German/English Salesperson as advertised on your website. **3**

As you can see from my attached CV, I am a German native speaker and I speak English almost fluently. I worked as a tour guide for Travel Tours in Germany. At the moment I am working for a travel agency, where I look after the computer bookings. **4**

The position that you are offering is just what I am looking for. I love working with people and I would like a job where I can use my English. **5**

My CV is attached. If you need more information, please let me know. **6**

I look forward to hearing from you. **7**

Yours sincerely **8**
Anna Bruckner **9**
Hauptstr. 16
45525 Hattingen
Germany
Home 0049 2324 4517…, Mobile 0049 172 3459933…
anna_bruckner@speednet…de

1	C
2	__
3	__
4	G
5	__
6	__
7	F
8	__
9	__

A abschließender Gruß
B Anrede
C Betreffzeile
D Grund des Schreibens

E Hinweis auf Anlagen
F Hoffnung auf Antwort
G kurze Erläuterung der eigenen Fähigkeiten

H Name und alle Kontaktdaten
I persönliche Motivation

salesperson
Verkaufsangestellte/r

skill
Fähigkeit, Fertigkeit

enthusiastic
engagiert

to be a team player
teamfähig sein

attached
beigefügt, angehängt

CV
Lebenslauf

advertised
ausgeschrieben

native speaker
Muttersprachler/in

almost
beinahe, fast

fluently
fließend

tour guide
Reiseleiter/in

travel agency
Reisebüro

booking
Buchung

Grammar: Sagen, wie man etwas tut   → **G12**

My English is fluent.   He's a terrible dancer.
I **speak** English fluent**ly**.   He **dances** terrib**ly**.

6 On the job

Nick and Liana. Read the statements.
Nick und Liana. Lesen Sie die Aussagen.

Hi. My name is Nick.
I'm a car mechanic.
I've just repaired
another car.

But I haven't phoned
the customer yet.
My hands are too dirty!

Hi. I'm Liana.
I'm a gardener.
I've just planted some
tomatoes.

But my boss hasn't
looked at them yet.
I hope it's all OK.

A **What are Nick and Liana talking about? Tick the right answer.**
Worüber sprechen Nick und Liana? Machen Sie ein Häkchen an die richtige Antwort.

Nick and Liana are talking about . . .

A ☐ their friends.   C ☐ their hobbies.

B ☐ their jobs.   D ☐ their dreams.

Vocabulary: Berufliche Tätigkeiten

answer the phone, clean rooms, cook meals, cut hair, drive trucks, feed animals,
help people, paint houses, plant flowers, repair cars, sell clothes, serve customers,
teach children, write emails

---

not yet
noch nicht

gardener
Gärtner/in

to plant
(ein)pflanzen

to serve
bedienen;
servieren

B **What about you? Finish the sentence with the right word.**
Und Sie? Vervollständigen Sie den Satz mit dem richtigen Wort.

cooked • driven • looked • painted • read • written

I've just _____ a text about Nick and Liana.

Ask Aysha

A **Listen to the radio show. What jobs do the three callers want to do? Tick the right three pictures.**

Hören Sie sich die Radiosendung an. Welche Berufe wollen die drei Anrufenden ausüben?
Machen Sie ein Häkchen an die drei passenden Bilder.

1  **2** 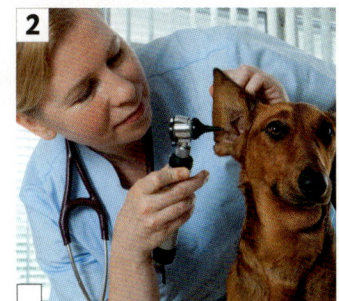 **3**  **4**

B **Listen to the radio show again. Tick *true* or *false* for sentences 1–3.**

Hören Sie sich die Radiosendung noch einmal an. Machen Sie bei den Sätzen 1–3 ein
Häkchen bei *richtig* oder *falsch*.

		true	false
1	Sally is interested in motorbikes.	☐	☐
2	Greg watches TV a lot.	☐	☐
3	Paula wants to be a chef.	☐	☐

Grammar: Was gerade (oder noch nicht) geschehen ist → **G 4**

regelmäßige Verben:
have (Kurzform **'ve**) oder **has** + Verb + **-ed**

I've just repaired a car.
Ich habe soeben ein Auto repariert.

unregelmäßige Verben:
have (Kurzform **'ve**) oder **has** + Verb
(Formen → vordere Umschlagseite, innen)

Leah hasn't written her application yet.
Leah hat ihre Bewerbung noch nicht
geschrieben.

C **On the job. Finish the sentences with the right verb.**

Bei der Arbeit. Vervollständigen Sie die Sätze mit dem richtigen Verb.

cooked • driven • finished • painted

1 "Murat, why haven't you cooked the chicken soup yet?"

  – "Because I've never _____ chicken soup before!"

2 "Jess, why aren't you painting that wall over there?"

  – "Because I haven't _____ this wall here yet!"

3 "Karel, have you _____ Mr Lee's car?"

  – "Yes, I've just finished it, boss."

4 "Have you _____ a truck before, Susan?"

  – "Of course I have! I'm a truck driver, boss!"

interested in
interessiert an

chef
Koch/Köchin

before
zuvor, schon
einmal

wall
Wand, Mauer

Dirty hands

. Monday. Another day at Newtown
. Motors. Another day as a car salesman.
. Simon had to read lots of emails, open
. doors, offer and serve coffee, take some
5 terrible drivers for test drives – but he
. didn't sell a car.

. Why not? Because he is a mechanic, not
. a car salesman! He thought back almost
. three months ago when his boss, Mrs
10 Grant, talked to him:

> **Mrs Grant**   Well, Simon, we're very
> pleased with your work. You're a good
> mechanic.
>
> **Simon**   Thanks, Mrs Grant. I like
> 15 my job. And I like helping people with
> their cars. I'm happy when the
> customers are happy.
>
> **Mrs Grant**   I know, Simon. Listen,
> our best salesman has just left us.
> 20 I've decided to give the job to our
> friendliest employee – you.
>
> **Simon**   That's very nice of you, Mrs
> Grant, but I really like repairing cars.
>
> **Mrs Grant**   But you'll love the job!
> 25 You're good with people, you're
> polite – and you won't have dirty hands
> any more! I'm sure your wife will be
> happy.

. No more dirty hands. That was true.
30 But also: no more talking to the other
. mechanics, no more trying to find the
. problem with an engine, no more helping
. car drivers. Now Simon had to tell
. people to give up their old car and buy a
35 new one. He even had to wear a suit!

When he came home that evening,   .
Julie, his wife, looked at him.   .

"You look happy," she said.   .
"Wait – you look like you've just sold   .
a car."   40

"No, I haven't," Simon answered.   .
"I'll never sell a car."   .

"What?" Julie didn't understand.   .

"I've just decided what to do," said Simon. .
"I'll tell Mrs Grant that I want to repair 45
cars again. That's what I'm good at. That's .
what I'm happy with. And I hope you   .
won't mind the dirty hands again."   .

"Your dirty   .
hands?" Julie said. 50
"Darling,
I married a car
mechanic,   .
not a salesman!"   .

---

car salesman
Autoverkäufer

test drive
Probefahrt

**(three months)
ago**
vor (drei Monaten)

pleased
zufrieden

**left (Grundform:
to leave)**
verlassen

to decide
(sich) entscheiden

employee
Angestellte/r

wife
Ehefrau

engine
Motor; Maschine

even
sogar

to marry
heiraten

to deal with
sich kümmern um

Vocabulary: Was auf der Arbeit zu tun ist

mit Dingen: check something, deal with something, organize something, plan something, present something, recommend something, translate something, work on something
mit Menschen: drive somebody, help somebody, listen to somebody, look after somebody, meet somebody, phone somebody, talk to somebody, tell somebody, thank somebody

A **Write sentences. Use all the words.**
Schreiben Sie Sätze. Benutzen Sie alle Wörter.

> **Skills Tip**
>
> Jeder Satz fängt mit einem Großbuchstaben an und hört mit einem Punkt auf.

1 drivers / has to take / A / test drives. / car salesman / for

_____

2 people / with their cars. / likes / helping / Simon

_____

3 that / a car. / thinks / His wife Julie / he has just sold

_____

4 a car mechanic / he has decided / But / again. / to be

_____

B **Who is talking – Simon, Julie or Mrs Grant? Write the name behind the statement.**
Wer spricht – Simon, Julie oder Mrs Grant? Schreiben Sie den Namen hinter die Aussage.

1 "Every man should have clean hands – always." _____

2 "It's so good to see you happy again!" _____

3 "Don't worry. I'm sure we'll be able to repair it." _____

> **Grammar: *many* (= viele) und *much* (= viel)**
>
> **I always get too many emails.**
> Ich bekomme immer zu viele Emails.
>
> **I don't have much time.**
> Ich habe nicht viel Zeit.

C **Simon's job. Circle the right word. The Grammar box above can help you.**
Simons Job. Umkringeln Sie das richtige Wort. Der *Grammar*-Kasten oben kann Ihnen helfen.

1 How many / much money do you want to spend on your new car?

2 Well, I'm new in this job. I haven't sold many / much cars yet.

3 Not many / much customers really want to buy a car. They just want to go for a test drive.

4 Working as a salesman isn't many / much fun for me. I want to work as a mechanic again.

to be able
in der Lage sein

Ziel: Ich kann meine Meinung sagen und Vorschläge machen.

My problem at work

Samantha Hobart has got a problem. She discusses it with her social network friends.

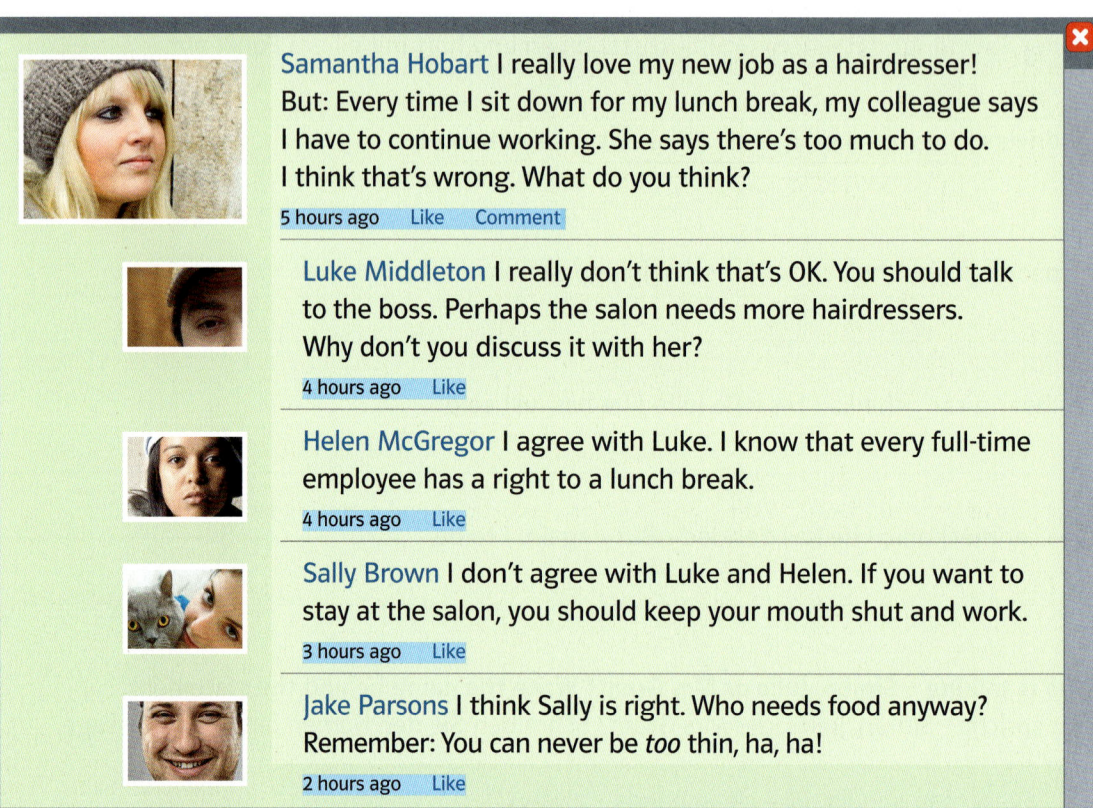

> **Samantha Hobart** I really love my new job as a hairdresser! But: Every time I sit down for my lunch break, my colleague says I have to continue working. She says there's too much to do. I think that's wrong. What do you think?
> 5 hours ago   Like   Comment

> **Luke Middleton** I really don't think that's OK. You should talk to the boss. Perhaps the salon needs more hairdressers. Why don't you discuss it with her?
> 4 hours ago   Like

> **Helen McGregor** I agree with Luke. I know that every full-time employee has a right to a lunch break.
> 4 hours ago   Like

> **Sally Brown** I don't agree with Luke and Helen. If you want to stay at the salon, you should keep your mouth shut and work.
> 3 hours ago   Like

> **Jake Parsons** I think Sally is right. Who needs food anyway? Remember: You can never be *too* thin, ha, ha!
> 2 hours ago   Like

A   **What are Samantha's friends saying? Tick *true* or *false* for sentences 1–4.**
Was sagen Samanthas Freunde/Freundinnen? Machen Sie bei den Sätzen 1–4 ein Häkchen bei *richtig* oder *falsch*.

		true	false
1	Luke: Perhaps the salon hasn't got enough hairdressers.	☐	☐
2	Helen: Every employee can have a lunch break.	☐	☐
3	Sally: You should talk about it.	☐	☐
4	Jake: You need food.	☐	☐

B   **Match the entries 1–3 and the comments A–C. Draw lines.**
Ordnen Sie den Einträgen 1–3 die Kommentare A–C zu. Ziehen Sie Linien.

1   My colleagues shout at me.   A   You could get a driving licence.

2   I haven't got enough money.   B   Why don't you get a job?

3   I'm never allowed to drive the firm's car.   C   Perhaps you shouldn't wear earphones at work.

Vocabulary: Die eigene Meinung sagen und Vorschläge machen

Meinungen äußern: I (don't) think …	**Vorschläge machen:** Perhaps … /
Auf andere Meinungen reagieren:	Why don't you …? / You could … /
I (don't) agree … / … is / are right / wrong.	You should …

---

to continue working weiter arbeiten

perhaps vielleicht

salon Friseursalon

to agree zustimmen

full-time Ganztags-

right Recht

to keep your mouth shut den Mund halten

anyway überhaupt

thin dünn

allowed erlaubt

Ziel: Ich kann über die Arbeit in verschiedenen Firmenbereichen sprechen.

Inside the firm

A **Where do they work? Read statements 1–6 and match the English words for the parts of a firm to the German words A–F.**
Wo arbeiten sie? Lesen Sie die Aussagen 1–6 und ordnen Sie den englischen Wörtern für Firmenbereiche die deutschen Wörter A–F zu.

1 I'm good with my hands and I want to produce things so I work in **production**. __B__

2 I'm good at drawing technical things. That's why I work in **design**. _____

3 I've always been good at selling things to people so I work in **sales**. _____

4 I'm polite and I'm good at talking to people. I work in the **reception**. _____

5 I like sorting things and I don't like sitting around so I work in the **post room**. _____

6 I like eating – so I'm happy working in the **canteen**! _____

A Empfang
B Fertigung
C Kantine
D Konstruktion
E Poststelle
F Vertrieb

B **Luke is taking a group of pupils on a tour of the firm.**
Put in the parts of the firm that he is describing.
Look at A again if you need help.
Luke macht mit einer Schülergruppe einen Rundgang durch die Firma. Fügen Sie die Firmenbereiche ein, die er beschreibt. Schauen Sie sich A noch einmal an, wenn Sie Hilfe brauchen.

Good morning and welcome to our tour of the firm.

We start with the biggest place here. It's where everything is

produced, so it's called _____ [1].

Next we'll have a quick look at the room where all

the new technical things are drawn. It's called

_____ [2]. And next you can have

a look at the _____ [3]

where all our many letters and parcels are sorted.

And you'll all love the following place. Are you hungry?

It's where our meals are cooked – the _____ [4]!

to produce
herstellen, produzieren

to draw
zeichnen

technical
technisch

that's why
deshalb

to sort
sortieren

welcome
willkommen

parcel
Paket

Grammar: Sagen, was getan wird   ↗ **G 8**

An advert **is written**.	Letters **are sorted**.
Eine Anzeige wird geschrieben.	Briefe werden sortiert.

7 Let's go!

Ziel: Ich kann über Pläne und Absichten sprechen. *Beispiel: I'm going to find a new job.*

After school. Read the dialogue.
Nach der Schule. Lesen Sie das Gespräch.

Kate

Kerim

1. Hi Kerim. School is almost over. What are you going to do after school?

Hi Kate. I'm going to drive a truck through Europe in the summer. What about you and Leo?

2. We're going to go to Sweden for a few months.

Really? Cool. What are you going to do there?

3. I'm going to work in a restaurant and Leo is going to work as a builder.

I see. Do you speak Swedish?

4. No, but most people there speak English. I'm really excited. I've always wanted to go abroad.

Yeah, well, I'm going to be in Spain a lot – in the truck, of course.

5. That sounds good too. Let's keep in touch, OK?

Sure. If I come to Sweden, I'll give you a call!

over vorbei	
through durch	
Europe Europa	
Sweden Schweden	
builder Bauarbeiter/in	
Swedish Schwedisch	
excited aufgeregt	
abroad im/ins Ausland	
to sound sich anhören	
to keep in touch in Kontakt bleiben	
to give somebody a call jemanden anrufen	

A **What's true? Tick the right statements.**
Was stimmt? Machen Sie ein Häkchen an die richtigen Aussagen.

A ☐ Kerim is going to work as a driver.
B ☐ Kate is going to go abroad.
C ☐ Kate speaks Swedish.
D ☐ Kerim is going to have a holiday in Spain.

Vocabulary: Im Gespräch reagieren

I see. – Listen, … – Really? – Sure. – That sounds good. – What about …? – Yeah, well …

B **What about you?**
Und Sie?

I'm going to work as a _____.

I'd like to work in _____.

Poland *Croatia* *Italy* *Lithuania* *Slovenia* *Portugal*

Going abroad for work

A   **Listen to the phone call. How is Nils travelling to Manchester? Tick the two right pictures.**

A2.9   Hören Sie sich das Telefongespräch an. Wie reist Nils nach Manchester? Machen Sie ein Häkchen an die beiden passenden Bilder.

B   **Listen to the phone call again. Tick A or B for sentences 1–4.**

Hören Sie sich das Telefongespräch noch einmal an. Machen Sie bei den Sätzen 1–4 ein Häkchen bei A oder B.

1   **Nils is starting a new job in**

    A ☐ England.
    B ☐ Sweden.

2   **Nils is going to work**

    A ☐ in a hospital.
    B ☐ in a restaurant.

3   **Sandra tells Nils to**

    A ☐ drive carefully.
    B ☐ have breakfast first.

4   **Nils is going to drive**

    A ☐ on the left.
    B ☐ on the right.

Grammar: Pläne und Absichten   → G 6

I'm going to work as a hairdresser.   **Sue is going to go abroad.**
Ich werde als Friseur/in arbeiten.   Sue hat vor, ins Ausland zu gehen.

C   **Plans. Choose the right verb and circle it.**

Pläne. Wählen Sie das richtige Verb und umkringeln Sie es.

1   First Nils is going to | find | | look | his new colleagues in the restaurant.

2   Then Sandra is going to | draw | | show | him his new flat.

3   They're all going to | have | | like | a meal together.

Grammar: Bedingungssätze   → G 9

If I get the new job, I'll earn more money. / I won't earn more money.
Wenn ich die neue Stelle bekomme, verdiene ich mehr Geld. / nicht mehr Geld.

D   **What if …? Finish the if-sentences. Use *will/'ll* 😊 or *won't* 😞 .**

Was ist, wenn …? Vervollständigen Sie die if-Sätze. Benutzen Sie *will/'ll* 😊 oder *won't* 😞 .

1   I like going to other countries.   😊   If I find a job abroad, I _____ leave Germany.

2   An English firm has offered me a job.   😊   If I take it, they _____ pay for my flat.

3   I'm glad I can speak English.   😞   If I need a holiday job abroad, I _____ have

problems finding one.

glad
froh

Immigrants are important to our town

by Rebecca Carter

Life without immigrants would be different in our town – and not half as nice!

Bina Dinkar is a chef at the "Taj Mahal" Indian restaurant. She was a baby when she came to England. "My parents taught me to cook," says Bina. "And then I learned much more about food at college. Of course, we offer English food at the restaurant too. But most people who come to us want Indian food." Now, without Bina and her Indian food we would be – hungry!

Timo Roth is an electrician from Germany. He puts solar panels on English houses for a German company. "I love the weekends here. We all go out together," Timo says. Timo has got lots of friends here at the rugby club. "It said *Rugby Football Club* at the door," he told me. "I really wanted to play football, not rugby. But now I love the game." And our town loves you, Timo. You're our star player!

Nadja Jung is from Germany too. She works as a baker at Dobbs Bakery. Jim Dobbs says, "Everybody loves German bread. We have got this new bread now that we call 'Wunderbread'." And Nadja? "I love it here. The people are really nice and polite. And I love English toast and marmalade and a cup of tea in the mornings. Very good!" Yes, just like you, Nadja. Wunderbar!

Piotr Szwarc is a plumber from Poland. He likes England, but he gets angry sometimes: "People say that we don't speak English and take away jobs from English people." Unfortunately, Piotr is right. Yes, that IS what some people say … Piotr says, "Listen to me. I speak good English. And just look around you – there's enough work here for everybody." I know Piotr is right, because I needed a plumber but couldn't find one – until I met Piotr! We need you, Piotr. Please stay!

Line numbers: 5, 10, 15, 20, 25, 30, 35, 40, 45, 50, 55, 60, 65

Vocabulary: Ich bin … / Etwas ist …

I'm … angry, crazy, enthusiastic, excited, glad, hungry, interested, pleased, surprised.
Something is … allowed, attached, classy, clear, different, fast, furnished, hard, idiotic, necessary, real, required, short, special, thin, unusual, used.

---

immigrant
Immigrant/in,
Einwanderer/in

different
anders;
andere/r/s

Indian
indisch

electrician
Elektriker/in

solar panel
Sonnenkollektor

baker
Bäcker/in

marmalade
Marmelade aus
Zitrusfrüchten

plumber
Installateur/in,
Anlagenmecha-
niker/in für
Sanitär-,
Heizungs- und
Klimatechnik

Poland
Polen

A **Match the names A – D to the photos 1 – 4.**
Ordnen Sie die Namen A – D den Fotos 1 – 4 zu.

A Bina   **B** Nadja   **C** Piotr   **D** Timo

1

2

3

4

B **Who's talking? Choose the right person for sentences 1 – 4.**
Wer spricht? Wählen Sie die richtige Person für die Sätze 1 – 4.

Bina • Nadja • Piotr • Timo

1 "When my parents came to visit me here, they brought their own bread!" _____

2 "I love going out to the pub with my friends after a game." _____

3 "Our most popular meal is 'Chicken Tikka Masala', of course." _____

4 "I work all the time, so I really don't have time for hobbies." _____

C **Find the right word in the text for definitions 1 – 3.**
Finden Sie zu den Worterklärungen 1 – 3 das passende Wort im Text.

1 Eine Person, die in ein Land kommt, um dort zu bleiben: _____

2 Englischer Brotaufstrich aus Zitrusfrüchten: _____

3 Eine Person, die sich in Badezimmern gut auskennt: _____

D **Rebecca's plans. Finish the sentences with the right going to-form.**
Rebeccas Pläne. Vervollständigen Sie die Sätze mit der richtigen *going to*-Form.

1 My boyfriend and I _____ live in the USA.

2 He _____ look for a job there soon.

3 He's a chef so it _____ be easy for him.

4 But before that, I _____ write a few more newspaper articles

and earn some money!

own
eigene/r/s

Ziel: Ich kann einem Text die wichtigsten Informationen entnehmen.

In England

Tip: You don't have to understand every word.

· If you come to England, you'll see that most
· English people are very friendly. But things
· will be easier for you if you know a little bit
· about some English customs. No problem!
5 The most important thing is to be polite.
· Always. Just say "please", "thank you" and
· "sorry" as often as you can.

And then there's queuing. In England, more
than two people will always form a queue.
Join them – at the end, of course! Now you 10
can even try and talk to the person in front
of you.

All English people love small talk! Just say
some sentences about the weather, the
traffic, TV or sports. If you know the person, 15
use his or her first name.

This is also very English, by the way:
Everybody uses first names. Most of the time,
employees even call their boss by his or her
first name! That does not always mean that 20
they're good friends …

And finally another important English custom:
the After-Work-Drink. Colleagues go to the
pub after work to have a drink together.
Sounds great, doesn't it? And it's fun! But you 25
have to know that people buy each other
"rounds". Also, no server will come to serve
your pints of beer or glasses of wine. You go
to the bar, ask for the drinks, pay for them
and take them back to your colleagues' table. 30
Easy, really – and very polite!

---

custom
Sitte, Brauch, Gepflogenheit, Gewohnheit

queuing; queue
Schlange stehen; (Warte-)Schlange

to form
bilden

to join
(sich) anschließen

small talk
Geplauder

traffic
Verkehr

first name
Vorname

by the way
übrigens

another
ein/e andere/r/s

to buy a round
eine Runde ausgeben

pint
„Halbe"
(0,568 Liter)

A **What is the text about in general? Tick the best summary.**
Wovon handelt der Text ganz allgemein? Machen Sie ein Häkchen an die beste Zusammenfassung.

The text is about …

A ☐ the mistakes that tourists to England often make.
B ☐ English customs that visitors to England should know about.
C ☐ how to find a job in an English pub.

B **Tick the five important English customs that the text talks about.**
Machen Sie ein Häkchen an die fünf wichtigen englischen Gepflogenheiten, die im Text erwähnt werden.

1 ☐ being open
2 ☐ buying rounds
3 ☐ using first names
4 ☐ looking smart
5 ☐ queuing
6 ☐ using small talk
7 ☐ playing sports
8 ☐ being polite

C **1** **Explain three of the customs in German.**
Erklären Sie drei der Gepflogenheiten auf Deutsch.

2 **Explain two of the customs in English.**
Erklären Sie zwei der Gepflogenheiten auf Englisch.

Ziel: Ich kann vom Englischen ins Deutsche vermitteln.

In Japan

Lesen Sie die Erläuterungen einer Engländerin über wichtige japanische Gepflogenheiten und fassen Sie sie knapp auf Deutsch zusammen.

1 I was quite surprised at how polite Japanese people are. Politeness is even more important than in England! You just cannot be too polite in Japan.

Das Wichtigste ist: Seid immer _____.

2 Most Japanese people know that Europeans normally shake hands when they meet. But shaking hands isn't the custom in Japan. People – men and women – bow instead. Careful: Don't hit the other person's head!

Gebt Japanern nicht die Hand zur Begrüßung, sondern

_____.

3 If you're invited to somebody's home, you'll have to take off your shoes and leave them in the front area before you go in. So don't wear socks that have got holes in them!

Wenn ihr bei jemandem zu Hause eingeladen seid, müsst ihr beim Eintreten

_____.

4 The Japanese love presents. Always take a present when you're invited to somebody's home. It shouldn't be expensive, though.

Wenn ihr bei jemandem zu Hause eingeladen seid, solltet ihr _____

_____.

5 Now this is interesting as well: I don't know why, but if you give or receive something (a present or a business card), always use both your hands!

Wenn ihr etwas überreicht oder in Empfang nehmt, benutzt immer

_____.

6 You should never eat or drink while you're walking down the street in Japan. It's not polite. If you're really hungry or thirsty, use a vending machine and stand next to the machine to eat or drink what you bought.

In Japan gilt es als unhöflich, im Gehen etwas _____

_____.

surprised überrascht	
normally normalerweise	
to shake hands Hände schütteln, sich die Hand geben	
to bow sich verbeugen	
instead stattdessen	
to hit stoßen, treffen	
to take off ausziehen	
hole Loch	
business card Visitenkarte	
both beide	

Grammar: Über Tätigkeiten sprechen   ↗ **G 15**

Shaking hands is a German custom.   **Being** polite is important in England.
Das Händeschütteln ist ein deutscher Brauch.   In England ist es wichtig, höflich zu sein.

Seitdem Lisa einen LKW fährt, spricht sie öfter Englisch. Warum?

I'm a truck driver and I love my job. I always knew that I wanted to become a driver. At first I only drove vans. I delivered parcels. After that I drove my first truck for a local furniture shop. It's not as easy as you think – all those narrow streets! Now I'm a long distance trucker. That was always my dream. It's really cool. And it's good that I can speak a little English because I have to talk to customs' people in other countries. And of course I want to talk to truckers from other countries too.

dustcart

Berufskraftfahrer/innen fahren viele verschiedene Fahrzeuge ...

dump truck

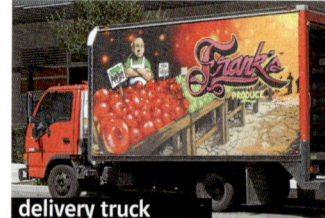

delivery truck

So you want to be a dump truck driver in the Australian mining industry? Read this:

➕ Good points:
– You don't have to be very fit.
– You can earn a lot of money.
– It's for men *and* women.

➖ Bad points:
– It's boring work: You drive up and down a big hole all day.
– 12-hour-days are normal.
– You're in the middle of nowhere.

bus

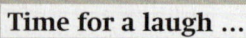

tow truck

Time for a laugh ...

A policeman stopped a truck driver and said, "You're the winner of our Safest Driver Contest. Well done! You win £3,000. What are you going to do with the money?"
"Hm, perhaps I should finally get a driving licence", the truck driver answered.

Well, I'd rather drive an Australian road train!

Ohne Englisch geht als Kellner gar nichts, findet Pjeter, denn …

Here in the Black Forest, lots of guests are tourists from other countries. Not many of them speak German, but most of them speak at least a little English. So if I want to do a good job, I have to give them information and advice in English. Luckily we've got an English language menu in the restaurant. But some people also ask for travel information ("How far is it to …?") or hiking recommendations ("Where can we go for a long but easy walk?"). And in this job, it's a good idea to be polite and answer the guests' questions: People often give you a bigger tip* if you're friendly!

* **tip** a little extra money that you give to somebody, for example somebody who serves you in a restaurant

A job in a restaurant is all about team work …

… and it isn't always glamourous.

But if you like people, you'll have fun every day (see below).

The stupidest thing I've ever heard from a guest: "Can you make sure there's no chocolate on my pizza? I'm allergic to chocolate." Chocolate on a pizza?? How do you react to this, if you still want a good tip? Easy – just stay cool and say: "Certainly, Madam. I'll tell the chef*."

* **chef** a cook in a restaurant, hotel, etc.

Did you know?

Nobody gives tips in Japan.

A lot of servers have to wear a kind of smart uniform. Sometimes it's a "dirndl".

Most waiters hate fast food restaurants.

"A photo of Joyce and me in the new restaurant. The food was good, but the service was really slow!"

serve • service • server
server = **waiter** (male)
waitress (female)

49

Elena arbeitet in einer Großstadtpraxis und spricht jeden Tag Englisch …

I'm a real 'people person' and my job allows me to deal with new and interesting people from all over the world every day. The best part of my job is seeing that I'm really helping people. Often people are very nervous, because they don't feel well or they're in pain[1] and they're afraid. I learned that if I stay calm[2] and listen to them, I can make them feel better. I'm the best English speaker in this surgery[3], so I can often help. Of course I have to do medical things as well. That's OK with me. I think giving injections and assisting the doctor is more fun than working at the reception.

[1] **to be in pain** Schmerzen haben
[2] **calm** ruhig
[3] **surgery** 1. Praxis, 2. Operation

WARNING:
IF YOU DON'T LIKE THE SIGHT OF BLOOD THIS IS NOT THE RIGHT JOB FOR YOU!

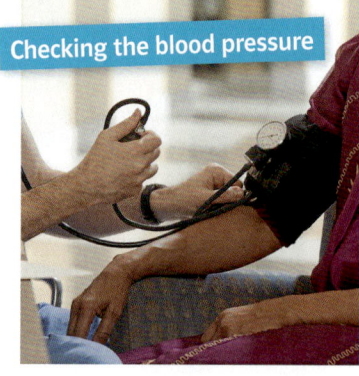

Checking the blood pressure

OUCH!

Giving injections

CLINIC RECEPTIONIST
PRIVATE PRACTICE FOR COSMETIC SURGERY IN LONDON

… The practice does not have a waiting room. The doctor's team of assistants has to make sure that our famous patients will not have to wait.

… We need someone who works well even when the clinic is extremely busy. You have to be a strong team player in our small team. …

Time for a laugh …

In the waiting room of a doctor's surgery
"Oh, hello, Mary. How are you?"
– "Hello, Sandy. I'm fine, thanks."

???   **Fine? Well, what is she doing in a doctor's surgery then?**

Different doctors:
general practitioner (GP)
paediatrician (children)
ear, nose and throat specialist
orthopaedic specialist
ophthalmologist (eyes)
dermatologist (skin)
dentist (teeth)
vet (animals)

doctor's surgery
doctor's practice
doctor's office
medical practice

Sebastian lebt in Australien und sucht sich seine Aufträge selbst …

I'm a qualified painter and decorator, trained and educated in Germany.

My services include: exterior and interior work on private houses, renovations to private/commercial buildings.

I am experienced, professional and my work is 100% customer-orientated.

I have my own tools[1] and van.

Please give me a call and ask for a quote[2]:
040556225 (Sebastian)

[1]| **tools** Werkzeuge
[2]| **quote** Angebot, Kostenvoranschlag

Some typical painting and decorating jobs:
- taking off old wallpaper and hanging new paper
- preparing wood, plaster, metal or other surfaces* for painting
- restoring old interior or exterior decor
- protecting surfaces from dirt and damp

*| **surface** Oberfläche

Before …   **… and after.**

Colours have the funniest names. Everybody knows **red**, **yellow** and **blue**.
You might even have heard of **magenta**.
But did you know **cayenne** or **ice**? And what name would you give **this colour**?

Kerim lernt wieder Englisch, denn er hat einen Plan …

I love being a painter and decorator, because the work is never boring. I work indoors and outdoors. I work on a building site[1], around a house or in the firm's workshop. Often I'm part of a team, but sometimes I don't see a colleague all day. Of course I have to use paintbrushes[2], but I have to deal with lots of different machines too. And I love the moment when the work is done. Everything looks nice and fresh and clean – and the customers are very happy! I'm learning English again at the moment because I want to go abroad for a while. Workers with my skills are wanted almost anywhere in the world.

[1]| **building site** Baustelle
[2]| **paintbrush** Pinsel

Mobiles

to **turn on**	einschalten, anmachen	↔ to turn off *(ausschalten)*
to **answer the phone**	ans Telefon gehen	↔ to phone/call/ring somebody *(jemanden anrufen)*
to **receive**	erhalten	↔ to send *(senden)*
to **text**	eine SMS-Nachricht verschicken, „simsen"	= to send a text
phone	Telefon	
mobile (phone)	Handy	! not "handy"
headphones	Kopfhörer	! a pair of headphones
earphones	Ohrhörer	! a pair of earphones
ringtone	Klingelton	→ to ring
text	SMS	→ to text

Free time

to **hang out**	„abhängen"	
to **surf the internet**	im Internet surfen	Emma often surfs the internet.
favourite	Lieblings-	Lady Gaga is my favourite singer.
to **go shopping**	einkaufen gehen	
to **watch TV**	fernsehen	My brother watches TV all the time.

At the hairdresser's

hairdresser	Friseur/in	→ hair
customer	Kunde/Kundin	
appointment	Termin, Verabredung	to make an appointment
coat	Mantel, Jacke	to wear a coat
to **curl**	kräuseln, aufdrehen	→ curly *(lockig)*
to **dry**	trocknen	→ dry *(trocken)*

Emails

subject	Betreff	
clear	klar, deutlich	
Yours sincerely	Mit freundlichen Grüßen	
rule	Regel, Vorschrift	to follow a rule *(eine Regel befolgen)*
joke	Witz	→ to joke *(einen Witz machen, scherzen)*

Internet forms

to **register (with)**	sich anmelden (bei)	
to **enter**	eingeben	↔ to delete *(löschen)*
to **tick**	ankreuzen, abhaken	
title	Anrede	
details	(Adress-)Daten, Angaben	
company	Firma	= firm
advertising	Werbung	→ advert *(Anzeige)*
field	Feld	
first name	Vorname	English people often use first names.
last name	Nachname, Familienname	
postcode	Postleitzahl	
phone number	Telefonnummer	
date of birth	Geburtstag	= birthday

Phrases

phrase	Redewendung, Ausdruck	
Well done!	Gut gemacht!	
all the time	die ganze Zeit	I listen to music all the time.

Symbole: = Synonym; ↔ Gegensatz; → Wortfamilie; ! Achtung

A Odd one out. Which word does not belong in the group? <u>Underline</u> it.
Welches Wort gehört nicht in die Gruppe? <u>Unterstreichen</u> Sie das Wort.

1 word • phrase • phone • sentence

2 receive • send • text • clean

3 cut • cry • curl • dry

B Pick the right phrase and write three answers.
Wählen Sie den richtigen Ausdruck und schreiben Sie drei Antworten.

Of course. • Thank you. • Good morning. • Well done!

1 I've passed my test. – _____

2 Can I have a cup of tea, please? – _____

3 Can I take your coat? – _____

C What's the word? Complete the words with the letters on the left.
Wie heißt das Wort? Vervollständigen Sie die Wörter mit den Buchstaben links.

1 CUTJEB   s_____

2 PMYAON   c_____

3 SSAIEERRD   h_____r

4 TMSUOE   c_____r

5 SREAH   p_____

6 TAIOUVR   f_____e

D Pick the right word in sentences 1–4 and circle it.
Wählen Sie das passende Wort in den Sätzen 1–4 und umkringeln Sie es.

1 Listen. I've got a new ringtone on my | headphones | | mobile phone | .

2 The | company | | customer | doesn't have an appointment.

3 No | jokes | | rules | in formal emails!

4 Tick this box if you want to | receive | | register | our newsletter.

E Complete the sentences with the right word or words.
Vervollständigen Sie die Sätze mit dem passenden Wort / den passenden Wörtern.

1 A _____ is a person who helps people look good.

2 You put "_____" at the end of an email.

3 The _____ was good when everybody laughs.

4 In an internet form, you have to _____ your details.

5 If you want to listen to the radio, you have to _____ it _____ first.

6 You wear a _____ in cold or rainy weather.

Friends

gender	Geschlecht	
male	männlich	↔ female
female	weiblich	↔ male
to **make friends**	Freundschaften schließen	→ to be friends (befreundet sein)
friendship	Freundschaft	→ friend
relationship	Beziehung	
boyfriend	(fester) Freund	↔ girlfriend
girlfriend	(feste) Freundin	↔ boyfriend
partner	Partner/in	
classmate	Klassenkamerad/in	→ class (Klasse)
interested in	interessiert an	→ interest (Interesse); interesting (interessant)
looking for	auf der Suche nach	→ to look for (suchen)
in touch	in Verbindung	Let's keep in touch.
to **share**	teilen	
to **understand**	verstehen	
feeling	Gefühl	→ to feel (fühlen)

Internet

site, website	Webseite	
social network	soziales Netzwerk	Do you use social networks?
community	Gemeinschaft	
profile	Profil, Selbstdarstellung	
wall	(Pinn-)Wand	
membership	Mitgliedschaft	→ member (Mitglied)
basic info	allgemeine Informationen	→ information
status	Status	
current location	derzeitiger Wohnort	
political views	politische Einstellung	
favourite	Lieblings-	
to **blog**	bloggen	→ blog
to **chat**	chatten	→ chat
to **download**	downloaden, herunterladen	to download a song from the internet
to **email/mail**	mailen	→ email/mail
to **post something**	etwas ins Internet stellen	
to **skype**	skypen	

Work

firm	Firma	= company, business
production	Produktion	→ to produce (herstellen)
canteen	Kantine	We have our lunch in the canteen.
lunch break	Mittagspause	→ lunch (Mittagessen)
job interview	Vorstellungsgespräch	to be invited for a job interview (zu einem Vorstellungsgespräch eingeladen sein)
boss	Chef/in	
colleague	Kollege, Kollegin	
customer	Kunde, Kundin	Always be polite to our customers!
reporter	Reporter/in	
machine operator	Maschinenführer/in	Alex works as a machine operator.
management assistant	Bürokauffrau/-mann	

Something is ...

classy	edel, elegant	a classy restaurant
crazy	verrückt	Are you crazy?
idiotic	idiotisch	an idiotic idea

Symbole: = Synonym;   ↔ Gegensatz;   → Wortfamilie;   **!** Achtung

A **Pick the right word ending (on the right) for each beginning (1–11) and write the words in your exercise book.**

Suchen Sie das richtige Wortende (rechts) für jeden Wortanfang (1–11) und schreiben Sie die Wörter in Ihr Heft.

1 boy…
2 class…
friend
3 friend…
mate
4 girl…
ship
5 inter…
6 loca…
site
7 member…
tion
8 net…
9 produc…
view
10 relation…
work
11 web…

B **Put in the English words for the German words.**

Tragen Sie die englischen Wörter für die deutschen Wörter (neben dem Rätsel) ein.

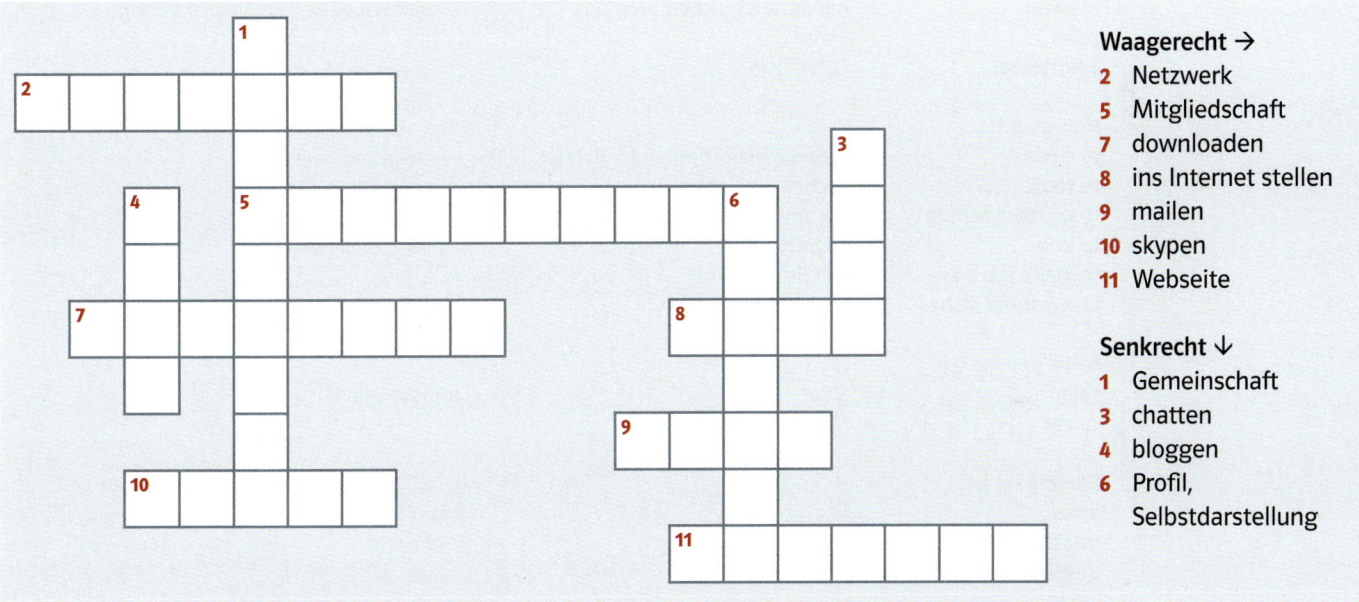

Waagerecht →
2 Netzwerk
5 Mitgliedschaft
7 downloaden
8 ins Internet stellen
9 mailen
10 skypen
11 Webseite

Senkrecht ↓
1 Gemeinschaft
3 chatten
4 bloggen
6 Profil, Selbstdarstellung

C **Complete the sentences with the right word from the word list "Work" on the left page.**

Vervollständigen Sie die Sätze mit dem richtigen Wort aus der Wortliste zu „Work" auf der linken Seite.

1 I work for a big _____. They make windows.

2 I'm a management assistant. I often have to talk to our _____s. It's fun.

3 I really like my _____ s. Most of them are my friends too.

4 We often go out after work. Sometimes our _____ comes with us!

5 Sandra and I usually have our _____ _____ together. But we don't go in the canteen.

6 But Sandra hopes that she can find a new job. Her first _____ _____ is next week.

Looking for a flat

flat	Wohnung	= apartment
a place of my own	meine eigene Bleibe	
to **move out**	ausziehen	→ to move (umziehen)
building	Gebäude	I like the colour of the building.
size	Größe	
neighbour	Nachbar/in	
advert	Anzeige	→ advertising (Werbung)

In the flat

furnished	möbliert	→ to furnish (möblieren)
furniture	Möbel	→ furnished
bed	Bett	→ bedroom (Schlafzimmer)
chair	Stuhl	
cupboard	Schrank	
shelf, shelves	Regal, Regale	
table	Tisch	= desk
oven	Backofen	Ben is taking the cookies out of the oven.
cable TV	Kabelfernsehen	
broadband	Breitband	
modern	modern	a modern flat
to **repair**	reparieren	↔ to break (kaputt machen)
to **paint**	malen, anstreichen	→ painter (Maler/in, Anstreicher/in)
paint	Farbe	
paintbrush	Farbpinsel	

Housework

to **clean**	saubermachen, reinigen, putzen	→ clean (sauber)
to **cook**	kochen	→ cook (Koch/Köchin)
to **do the washing**	die Wäsche machen	
to **iron**	bügeln	→ iron (Bügeleisen)
to **make the bed**	das Bett machen	
to **wash the dishes**	abwaschen, spülen	→ dishes (Geschirr)

Food

salad	Salat	tomato salad
carrot	Möhre, Karotte	

Something is ...

awful	furchtbar	= terrible
interesting	interessant	↔ boring
unusual	ungewöhnlich	→ usually

Phrases

What would you like?	Was wünschen Sie?
I'd like ...	Ich hätte gern ...
Anything else?	Noch etwas?
Here you are.	Hier, bitte.
How can I help you?	Kann ich Ihnen behilflich sein?

Time phrases

right now	im Augenblick	= at the moment
just	gerade, soeben	

Symbole: = Synonym; ↔ Gegensatz; → Wortfamilie; ! Achtung

A Find 10 words. They are all things in a flat.
Finden Sie 10 Wörter. Es sind alles Dinge in einer Wohnung.

F	R	O	P	S	E	C	Y	L	A	N	T	I	D	E	R
L	O	U	N	K	E	M	T	W	Z	Y	N	O	P	R	A
A	S	B	O	P	N	G	E	I	S	K	E	F	T	V	W
J	E	E	N	T	O	G	S	N	R	S	O	F	A	P	L
E	C	U	P	B	O	A	R	D	A	H	O	U	B	X	P
P	H	I	L	T	E	D	M	O	V	E	N	Z	L	U	C
K	A	N	D	E	Y	P	L	W	G	L	A	B	E	D	W
Y	I	N	T	R	I	K	T	E	R	F	R	O	P	O	H
G	R	A	U	N	S	K	Y	T	R	A	W	L	M	O	N
B	E	S	G	I	N	T	F	U	R	N	I	T	U	R	E
P	R	E	A	N	W	R	I	G	H	B	O	V	R	D	S

B What housework are these people doing? Look at the photos and complete sentences 1–6.
Welche Hausarbeit machen diese Menschen? Schauen Sie sich die Fotos an und vervollständigen Sie die Sätze 1–6.

1 Jamie is _____.

2 Maria is _____ the _____.

3 Tim is _____.

4 Cassie is _____ the kitchen.

5 Irina is _____ the _____.

6 Pedro is _____ the _____.

C Complete the questions.
Vervollständigen Sie die Fragen.

1 Wie fragen Sie, ob Sie einem Kunden behilflich sein können?

How _____?

2 Wie fragen Sie, ob der Kunde noch etwas wünscht?

Anything _____?

3 Was sagen Sie, wenn Sie dem Kunden das gewünschte Produkt zeigen.

Here _____?

Moving

on the move	in Bewegung	→ to move (*sich bewegen*)
driving lessons	Fahrstunden	
driving licence	Führerschein	
driving test	Führerscheinprüfung	to pass the driving test (*die Führerscheinprüfung bestehen*)
to **pass**	bestehen	↔ to fail (*durchfallen*)
public transport	öffentlicher Nahverkehr	to use public transport
flight	Flug	→ to fly
accident	Unfall	
to **drive**	(*selbst*) fahren	→ (bus/car/train) driver
to **fly**	fliegen	→ flight
to **cycle**, to **ride**	Rad fahren	→ cycling (*Radfahren*)
to **walk**	gehen	= to go on foot
to **rent**	mieten	→ rent (*Miete*)
to **get (to …)**	(nach …) kommen, gelangen	How do I get to London?
to **change trains**	umsteigen	
to **get off**	aussteigen	↔ to get in (the car), to get on (the bus, the train) (*einsteigen*)
to **crash the car into something**	mit dem Auto in etwas hineinkrachen	→ car crash (*Autounfall*)

Cars etc.

motorbike	Motorrad	to ride a motorbike
camper van	Wohnmobil	
lorry, truck	LKW	→ trucker (*LKW-Fahrer/in*)
van	(Klein-)Transporter	
jeep	Jeep	
bike	Fahrrad	
plane	Flugzeug	
train	Zug	The 8.48 train doesn't stop at Eastwood.
wreck	Wrack	
satnav	Satellitennavigationssystem, „Navi"	
(car) boot	Kofferraum	
used	gebraucht	↔ new

Giving directions

directions	Wegbeschreibung	to give somebody directions to something (*jemandem den Weg zu etwas beschreiben*)
you should	du solltest	
mustn't	nicht dürfen	
to **follow**	folgen, befolgen	to follow advice (*einen Rat befolgen*)
to **cross**	überqueren	to cross a street (*eine Straße überqueren*)
to **turn left/right**	links/rechts abbiegen	→ to turn around (*sich umdrehen*)
along	entlang	
around	in der Nähe	
between	zwischen	
in front of	vor	↔ behind
next to	neben	
opposite	gegenüber (von)	
right through	direkt durch	
straight ahead	geradeaus	Go straight ahead.

In town

church	Kirche	
department store	Kaufhaus	She works in a department store.
pub	Kneipe	
phone box	Telefonzelle	

Symbole: = Synonym;   ↔ Gegensatz;   → Wortfamilie;   **!** Achtung

A Whose are they? Match the owners (1–5) with the vehicles and complete the sentences.
Wem gehören sie? Ordnen Sie den Besitzern/Besitzerinnen (1–5) die Fahrzeuge zu und vervollständigen Sie die Sätze.

1
Ricky

2
Linda

3
Louis and Kim

4
Paula

5
Andrew

A

B

C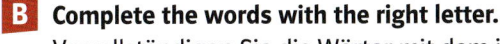

D

E

1 Ricky drives the _____. It's his job.

2 Linda rides her _____ in her free time.

3 Louis and Kim go on holiday in their _____.

4 Paula is tired. She drives her _____ all day.

5 Andrew often goes for long trips on his _____.

B Complete the words with the right letter.
Vervollständigen Sie die Wörter mit dem jeweils richtigen Buchstaben.

1 fl __ ght,   d __ rect __ ons

2 b __ __ t,   f __ ll __ w,   __ pp __ site

3 aro __ nd,   ch __ rch,   p __ b

4 b __ tw __ __ n,   cycl __,   wr __ ck

5 __ ccident,   __ long,   s __ tn __ v

C What do these words mean? Tick the right answer.
Was bedeuten diese Wörter? Machen Sie ein Häkchen an die richtige Antwort.

1 public transport:

A ☐ buses and trains which people use to travel

B ☐ a very long bus for many people

C ☐ lorries that everybody can use

2 department store:

A ☐ a small shop in a small town

B ☐ a big shop that sells many different things

C ☐ a shop that only sells very cheap things

3 satnav:

A ☐ a satnav plays music

B ☐ a satnav gives you directions

C ☐ a satnav washes the dishes

Applying for a job

advertised	ausgeschrieben	→ advert *(Anzeige)*; to advertise *(werben)*
to **apply (for)**	sich bewerben (um)	→ application
application	Bewerbung	→ to apply
apprenticeship	Lehre, Ausbildung	to do an apprenticeship *(eine Ausbildung machen)*
position	(Arbeits-)Stelle	= job
dream job	Traumberuf	Chauffeur is my dream job.
skill	Fähigkeit, Fertigkeit	→ skilled *(ausgebildet, qualifiziert)*
CV	Lebenslauf	
job interview	Vorstellungsgespräch	to invite someone to a job interview *(jemanden zum Vorstellungsgespräch einladen)*
to **be good at**	etwas gut können	I'm very good at looking after children.
enthusiastic	engagiert	
to **be a team player**	teamfähig sein	
to **be able**	in der Lage sein	= can
to **recommend**	empfehlen	
attached	beigefügt, angehängt	→ to attach *(beifügen, anhängen)*

Jobs

(shop) assistant	Verkäufer/in	to work as a shop assistant
car mechanic	Automechaniker/in	
chauffeur	Chauffeur/in, Fahrer/in	
personal assistant	persönliche/r Assistent/in	
salesperson	Verkaufsangestellte/r	→ to sell *(verkaufen)*
singer	Sänger/in	→ to sing *(singen)*
tour guide	Reiseleiter/in	

Language skills

language	Sprache	
native speaker	Muttersprachler/in	→ to speak *(sprechen)*
fluently	fließend	
to **sound**	sich anhören	→ sound *(Klang)*

Clothes

look	Aussehen	→ to look
suit	Anzug; Kostüm	to wear a suit *(einen Anzug tragen)*
blouse	Bluse	
skirt	Rock	
shirt	Hemd	
tie	Krawatte	
leather shoes	Lederschuhe	
coat	Mantel, Jacke	
smart	schick	a smart shirt *(ein schickes Hemd)*
to **wear**	anziehen, tragen	
to **suit somebody**	jemandem gut stehen	The shirt suits you.

Phrases

I would	ich würde
if I were you, I'd …	an Ihrer Stelle würde ich …
to **look forward**	sich darauf freuen, von … zu hören
to hearing from …	

Symbole: = Synonym;   ↔ Gegensatz;   → Wortfamilie;   ! Achtung

A **What are these people wearing? Write the words for the clothes on the lines.**
Was haben diese Menschen an? Schreiben Sie die Wörter für die Kleidungsstücke auf die Linien.

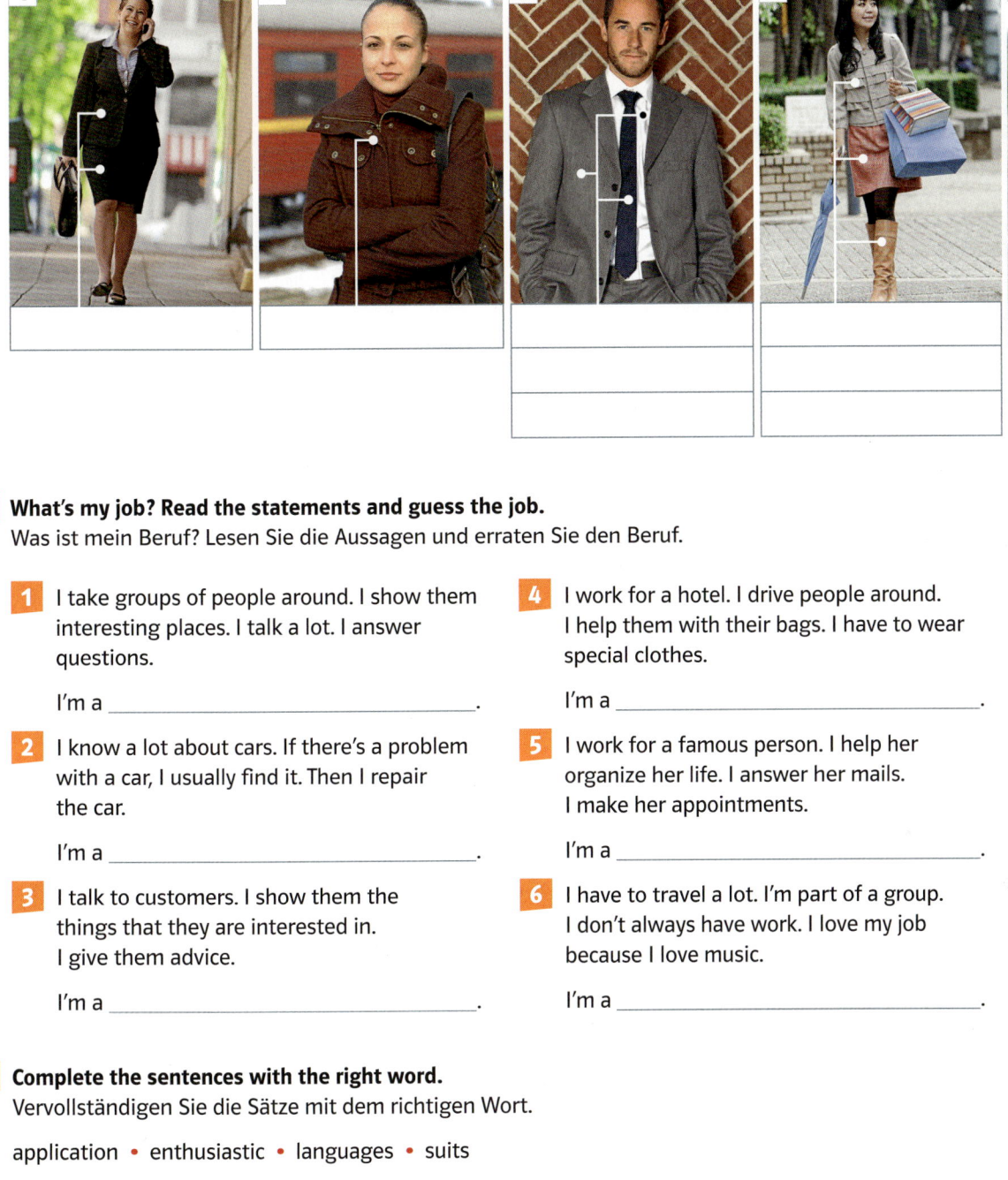

B **What's my job? Read the statements and guess the job.**
Was ist mein Beruf? Lesen Sie die Aussagen und erraten Sie den Beruf.

1 I take groups of people around. I show them interesting places. I talk a lot. I answer questions.

I'm a _____.

2 I know a lot about cars. If there's a problem with a car, I usually find it. Then I repair the car.

I'm a _____.

3 I talk to customers. I show them the things that they are interested in. I give them advice.

I'm a _____.

4 I work for a hotel. I drive people around. I help them with their bags. I have to wear special clothes.

I'm a _____.

5 I work for a famous person. I help her organize her life. I answer her mails. I make her appointments.

I'm a _____.

6 I have to travel a lot. I'm part of a group. I don't always have work. I love my job because I love music.

I'm a _____.

C **Complete the sentences with the right word.**
Vervollständigen Sie die Sätze mit dem richtigen Wort.

application • enthusiastic • languages • suits

1 The job advert sounds really interesting. I'm going to send the firm my

_____ soon.

2 My friend loves his job with the children. He's so _____, he

only talks about the job now.

3 You speak three _____ fluently – it's going to be easy for

you to find a job as a tour guide.

4 The suit that you're going to wear for the job interview _____ you a lot.

Talking

conversation	Gespräch	= talk, dialogue
statement	Aussage	
to **discuss**	diskutieren	→ discussion
to **agree**	zustimmen	↔ to disagree (*anderer Meinung sein*)
to **mind**	etwas dagegen haben	
to **decide**	(sich) entscheiden	→ decision (*Entscheidung*)
to **promise**	versprechen	→ promise (*Versprechen*)
to **depend**	darauf ankommen	
to **keep your mouth shut**	den Mund halten	
that's why	deshalb	

The world of work

full-time	Ganztags-	→ half-time (*Halbtags-*)
right	Recht	to be right (*recht haben*)
employee	Angestellte/r	
gardener	Gärtner/in	→ garden
chef	Koch/Köchin	= cook
to **continue working**	weiter arbeiten	

What people do at work

to **deal with**	sich kümmern um	
to **produce**	herstellen, produzieren	→ production
to **serve**	bedienen; servieren	→ server (*Servierer/in, Kellner/in*)
to **plant**	(ein)pflanzen	→ plant (*Pflanze*)
to **sort**	sortieren	
to **look after**	betreuen	
to **repair**	reparieren	
to **answer the phone**	ans Telefon gehen	
to **draw**	zeichnen	→ drawing (*Zeichnung*)
to **cook (meals)**	kochen	

Somebody is …

pleased	zufrieden	
glad	froh	
surprised	überrascht	→ surprise (*Überraschung*)
thin	dünn	↔ fat (*dick*)
welcome	willkommen	

Cars

car driver	Autofahrer/in	
test drive	Probefahrt	
engine	Motor; Maschine	
technical	technisch	
technology	Technologie	→ technical

Parts of a firm

production	Fertigung
design	Konstruktion
sales	Vertrieb
reception	Empfang
post room	Poststelle
canteen	Kantine

Time phrases

before	zuvor, schon einmal
a few months ago	vor ein paar Monaten

Symbole: = Synonym;   ↔ Gegensatz;   → Wortfamilie;   ! Achtung

A **Pick the right beginning and complete the verbs (1–9).**
Wählen Sie den richtigen Wortanfang aus und vervollständigen Sie die Verben (1–9).

re • de • dis • pro

1 _____mise

2 _____cide

3 _____duce

4 _____cuss

5 _____pend

6 _____pair

B **Match the verbs with the nouns.**
Ordnen Sie den Nomen die Verben zu.

If you …   you work in …

1 produce things	A sales.
2 draw technical things	B the canteen.
3 like eating	C production.
4 sell things to people	D the reception.
5 sort things	E the post room.
6 are good at talking to people	F design.

C **What are these people? Fill in the words (adjectives).**
Was sind diese Menschen? Tragen Sie die Eigenschaftswörter ein.

1 ___ ___ ___ ___ r ___ ___ ___ ___   **2** _____   **3** _____ s

D **Conversations. Match the two parts of the conversations (1–4 and A–C).**
Gespräche. Ordnen Sie die zwei Teile (1–4 und A–C) der Gespräche einander zu.

1 "I think the firm is getting too big."	A "Good idea. Let's discuss it with the others."
2 "Can't we work more on Mondays and less on Fridays?"	B "Yes, I agree."
3 "If you're late again tomorrow, you will have to go!"	C "Sorry, I haven't decided yet."
4 "Are you going to come with us to the pub later or not?"	D "It won't happen again. I promise."

Going abroad

abroad	im/ins Ausland	to go abroad (*ins Ausland gehen*)
immigrant	Immigrant/in, Einwanderer/in	→ to immigrate (*einwandern*)
custom	Sitte, Brauch, Gewohnheit, Gepflogenheit	
different	anders; andere/r/s	↔ same
another	ein/e andere/r/s	
to **become**	werden	
to **join**	(sich) anschließen	
to **marry**	heiraten	
to **keep in touch**	in Kontakt bleiben	
to **give somebody a call**	jemanden anrufen	= to phone/ring/call somebody
Europe	Europa	→ European (*europäisch*)
Sweden	Schweden	→ Swedish
Swedish	Schwedisch	→ Sweden
Italy	Italien	→ Italian (*Italienisch*)
Spain	Spanien	→ Spanish (*Spanisch*)
Poland	Polen	→ Polish (*Polnisch*)
Indian	indisch	→ India (*Indien*)
travel agency	Reisebüro	→ to travel (*reisen*)
booking	Buchung	→ to book (*buchen*)

Customs

queuing; queue	Schlange stehen; (Warte-)Schlange	
to **form**	bilden	
small talk	Geplauder	= conversation
first name	Vorname	↔ last name (*Nachname*)
to **buy a round**	eine Runde ausgeben	
to **shake hands**	Hände schütteln, sich die Hand geben	
to **bow**	sich verbeugen	
to **take off**	ausziehen	↔ to put on

Jobs

builder	Bauarbeiter/in	→ to build (*bauen*)
baker	Bäcker/in	→ to bake (*backen*)
plumber	Installateur/in, Anlagenmechaniker/in für Sanitär-, Heizungs- und Klimatechnik	
electrician	Elektriker/in	→ electric (*elektrisch*)

Somebody or something is ...

excited	aufgeregt	→ exciting (*aufregend*)
hard	hart	↔ soft (*weich*)
possible	möglich	↔ impossible (*unmöglich*)
necessary	nötig	
enough	genug	
special	besondere/r/s	

Food and drink

marmalade	Marmelade aus Zitrusfrüchten	! jam (*Marmelade*)
canned soup	Suppe aus der Dose	
alcohol	Alkohol	
smell	Geruch	→ to smell (*riechen*)

Phrases

Really?	Tatsächlich?
Sure.	Sicher.
I see.	Ich verstehe.
That sounds good.	Das hört sich gut an.

Symbole: = Synonym;   ↔ Gegensatz;   → Wortfamilie;   ! Achtung

A Take one piece out of each box of letters and put eight words together.
Nehmen Sie ein Teil aus jedem Buchstabenkasten und fügen Sie acht Wörter zusammen.

mar	al	nec	po	ex	elec	ag	an
ssi	ci	ma	en	co	tric	oth	ess
ted	ble	lade	cy	ary	er	ian	hol

1 marmalade
2
3
4
5
6
7
8

B What are these flags? Read sentences 1–8 carefully and finish them.
Was sind dies für Flaggen? Lesen Sie die Sätze 1–8 genau und vervollständigen Sie die Sätze.

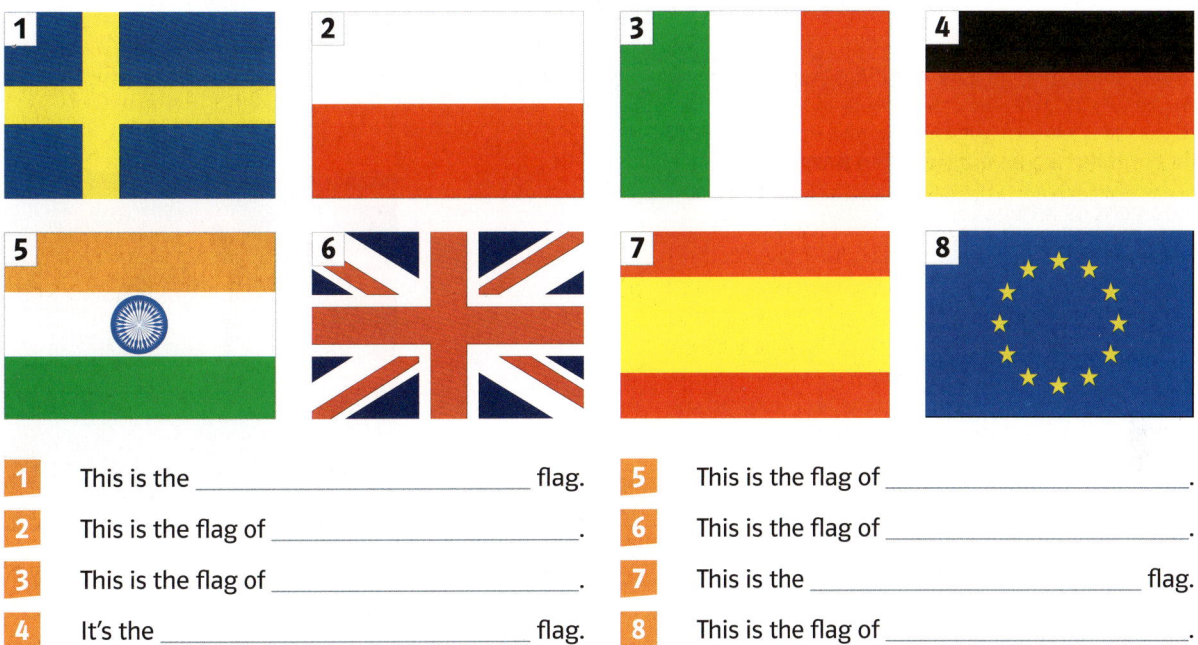

1 This is the _____ flag.
2 This is the flag of _____.
3 This is the flag of _____.
4 It's the _____ flag.
5 This is the flag of _____.
6 This is the flag of _____.
7 This is the _____ flag.
8 This is the flag of _____.

C Complete the sentences with the right word.
Vervollständigen Sie die Sätze mit dem richtigen Wort.

1 When a person comes into a country and wants to stay there, he or she often is an _____.

2 When something is not like other things, you call it _____.

3 A lot of people _____ when they know that they want to be together for a very long time.

4 In Britain you join a _____ when you have to wait together with other people.

5 When people just talk about the weather or sports, you call the conversation "_____".

6 A _____ is a person who repairs showers, for example.

Video lounge

Cheerleader auditions ◎ V1 **B B C** Motion Gallery

A **Bevor Sie sich das Video ansehen: Was denken Sie, ist Sport bei amerikanischen Studenten sehr beliebt?**

A ☐ Ja.   B ☐ Nein.

B **Nach dem Ansehen des Videos: Machen Sie ein Häkchen an die richtige Antwort.**

1 Konnie möchte …

  A ☐ Trainerin

  B ☐ Cheerleaderin

  C ☐ Preisrichterin

    werden.

2 Konnie kommt aus Großbritannien. Sie ist zu Gast in …

  A ☐ Kanada.

  B ☐ Kolumbien.

  C ☐ Kalifornien.

Making music ◎ V2 **B B C** Motion Gallery

Machen Sie ein Häkchen an die richtigen Antworten.

1 Im Video geht es darum, …

  A ☐ wie man eine Band gründet.

  B ☐ wie ein Song entsteht.

2 Wir sehen …

  A ☐ einen Produzenten und eine Sängerin.

  B ☐ eine Bandleaderin und einen Sänger.

The Grand Canyon Skywalk ◎ V3 **B B C** Motion Gallery

A **Before you watch the video: Think about the question and answer it.**
Bevor Sie sich das Video ansehen: Denken Sie über die Frage nach und beantworten Sie sie.

Ist der Grand Canyon

A ☐ ein Naturwunder?

B ☐ ein Kulturdenkmal?

B **After watching the video: True or false?**
Nach dem Ansehen des Videos: Richtig oder falsch?

1 Tourists can look down at the canyon from a walkway.

  A ☐ true   B ☐ false

2 1200 people can use the walkway at the same time.

  A ☐ true   B ☐ false

You can walk over the canyon

Out and about in New York City · V4

What does the video NOT talk about? Tick one word in each group.
Was wird im Video NICHT erwähnt? Machen Sie ein Häkchen an ein Wort in jeder Gruppe.

1 A ☐ taxis
B ☐ buses
C ☐ subway trains

2 A ☐ maps
B ☐ directions
C ☐ satnavs

3 A ☐ water towers
B ☐ banks
C ☐ skyscrapers

typical New York?

Tim gets a job · V5

Read the questions and tick the right answer.
Lesen Sie die Fragen und machen Sie ein Häkchen an die passende Antwort.

1 Why does Tim apply for the job?

A ☐ He is bored with his old job.

B ☐ He hasn't got a job.

2 Why is the phone interview good news?

A ☐ It is easier than a personal interview.

B ☐ It means the people are interested in him.

London and the Tube · V6

Tick the right summary.
Machen Sie ein Häkchen an die passende Zusammenfassung.

A ☐ The Tube is a London underground station. It's always busy.
You have to stop the trains to do repairs.

B ☐ The Tube is the name for a special team of repairmen in London.
They put in new tracks at midnight.

C ☐ The Tube is the London underground train system. It's very old.
It can only be repaired at night.

WATERLOO

five past five

The wannabe · V7

Pick the right word and complete the sentences.
Wählen Sie das richtige Wort und vervollständigen Sie die Sätze.

audition • modelling agency • profile • talent

1 Murat applies to a famous _____.

2 Murat takes part in an _____ for young singers,

dancers and actors.

3 You need _____ if you want to become a star.

4 The woman in the agency thinks that Murat has got a beautiful _____

_____.

A 2.1   Unit 1   A bad day for BigDadDave

Here's a busy office. Lots of people work here. And here's Dave. He's 21. He likes music. He's a rapper in his free time. He always has his MP3 player with him. He listens to it on his way to the office every morning.

At work, he phones customers every day. He's usually very good at his job. Mr Taylor, the boss, is pleased with him. His colleagues like him too. They know he raps and they know his rapper name, BigDadDave. Everybody calls him BigDad. But today something terrible happens. Listen.

Dave	… know him maybe, but you no good to show me baby …
Mary	Hi, BigDad. You're late today. You must phone Ms Francis at the Tradex company right away.
Dave	Hi, Mary. Just let me listen to this song. Tradex can wait.
Mary	No, they can't. Phone them now, please. Mr Taylor is angry already.
Dave	OK, OK. … now you step back … … now listen to me: Yo, man!
Ms Francis	Who is this? Tell me who you are!
Dave	This is Dave McCoy from Grantly and Company. I want to …
Ms Francis	Be quiet. I'm phoning your boss – now.
Dave	Oh no!
Mary	What's the problem, BigDad?
Dave	Don't ask. I think I've got a new name.
Mary	A new name?
Dave	Yes. From now on you can call me BigBadDave.

A 2.2   Unit 2   Terrible Tom

The people who work at Barker's Garage are good colleagues. They often go out together after work. And they all get together when it's somebody's birthday – normally. Listen.

Tom	Sales department, Tom speaking. Hello.
Patty	Hello, Tom. It's Patty, your favourite colleague.
Tom	Oh, hello, Patty.
Patty	How are things? Do all your customers want to buy the new Invista?
Tom	Yes, they do. It's the best car in the world. And I'm the best salesman, of course.
Patty	Ha, ha! You're terrible, Tom. Listen. It's Melinda's birthday today and …

Tom	Melinda? Do I know her?
Patty	Yes, you do! Long, blonde hair – my friend Melinda.
Tom	Ah, THAT Melinda!
Patty	It's her birthday today, so there's a meeting in the canteen at 1 o'clock to give Melinda her birthday present and have lunch together. And tonight it's drinks in the pub.
Tom	OK, thanks, Patty. See you later.

Two o'clock in the canteen …

Tom	Oh there you all are! Er, happy birthday, er, …
Patty	Melinda.
Tom	… Melinda. Sorry I'm late.
Patty	Why didn't you come here earlier?
Tom	Well, what does a car salesman do? He sells cars! I've just sold another Invista.
Patty	That's great, Tom. Listen, everybody. Tom wants to celebrate the sale of another car and say sorry to Melinda for missing her birthday lunch. See you all for drinks at the pub at seven o'clock. And do you know who's paying, Tom?
Tom	Melinda?
Patty	No. You!

A 2.3   Unit 3   The pizza problem

Paul and Tina are colleagues in a big shop. It's Friday evening and they're cooking at Tina's place. Paul has brought two pizzas. Listen.

Tina	I'm making us a nice salad. Can you do the pizzas, please, Paul? The oven is on already.
Paul	Of course. I'm quite a good cook, you know.
Tina	OK, OK. Just hurry up, Paul. I'm very hungry. The salad won't be enough.
Paul	I'm reading what it says on the packet. OK. 200 degrees, 11 minutes. … In you go, pizzas.
Tina	Let's have a drink in the living room while we're waiting. Oh, and we have to talk about a birthday present for Harry. He'll be 21 next week.
Paul	21! You know, I've known him since he was 11. And now he's 21 … …
Paul	… in the mornings. Hey. Twenty minutes. Our pizzas are almost ready.
Tina	Twenty minutes?! Are you sure?
Paul	Well, it says twenty-one minutes on the packet actually.

Tina	Let me check the packet. – I knew it! It isn't 21, it's 11 minutes!
Paul	Oh no! Quick!
Tina	Too late. I'm opening all the windows. What a smell!
Paul	And I'll throw these black pizzas away. I'm so sorry. What was I thinking?
Tina	You were thinking about Harry's birthday – remember? I told you he's 21 on Saturday. I think it's time to make a phone call.
Paul	A phone call?
Tina	Yes, to the pizza service.

A2.5 Unit 4 Rent-a-Wreck

Mila	Hi, Sue! Are you back from your holiday already? How was it?
Sue	Have you got some time? Let's go into this café and I can tell you. It was quite exciting actually.
Mila	OK.
	…
Sue	… and poor Tim was in hospital. He couldn't pick me up, and he couldn't show me Colorado in his car. So there I was, all alone at Denver Airport. I didn't have a car. And I didn't have much money. So first of all I went to the car rental desk and asked for their smallest camper van. The price was terrible! So then I asked about a small car – and do you know what? They didn't have one! "We don't drive small cars out here," the man at the desk said.
Mila	Poor you.
Sue	Well, what could I do? I took a bus into downtown Denver and walked around. In a shabby little street I saw a garage. There was a sign outside that said "Don't pay full prices for a big, new rental car. Rent a Wreck!" – And that's what I did! I paid for two weeks' rental of a "wreck", a little car that looked really old and dirty.
Mila	And did you like the car?
Sue	Yes, I did. I got in and started driving. The engine was noisy and the car wasn't very fast, but the brakes worked well, so it was OK for me. First of all I went to Boulder to visit my brother Tim in hospital. He looked terrible. Both his legs were broken! "That must have been a bad accident. Were you driving your own car?" I asked him. And he said, "Yes, my brakes suddenly didn't work. That's the problem

with modern cars and their electronic systems." "That's terrible," I said. "I'm so glad that this can't happen to me – my rental car is from Rent-a-Wreck in Denver …"

A2.7 Unit 5 Forget the interview

Jenny Williams	Good morning. Metronorma, Human Resources Department.
Peter Townsend	Hi. It's about my interview.
Jenny Williams	And your name is …?
Peter Townsend	Pete, er, Peter, Peter Townsend.
Jenny Williams	And how can I help you, Mr Townsend.
Peter Townsend	Well, as I said, it's about my interview. It's on Friday.
Jenny Williams	Yes. I can see it on my computer screen. Friday, 9 a.m.
Peter Townsend	Well, that's the problem, you see. I don't know about your boss, Mr … eh … Williams, but I really wouldn't like an interview at 9 a.m. I'm usually still in bed then.
Jenny Williams	So you aren't good at working hard in the morning?
Peter Townsend	In the morning? Heavens no! I usually only get back from the pub at around midnight. And then I'm tired all day. But don't tell your boss that.
Jenny Williams	Don't tell my boss. I see.
Peter Townsend	So could you ask your boss if I could have the interview after 3 p.m.? That would be great. And what do you think I should wear? I was thinking of coming in jeans and a T-shirt – a clean one, of course. That will be OK, won't it? I just haven't got time to go out and buy a jacket and trousers.
Jenny Williams	Or even a suit?
Peter Townsend	A suit! Me in a suit? Never!
Jenny Williams	Well, I've got some news for you, Mr Townsend. You won't need a suit, you won't even need a clean T-shirt, because you won't have an interview on Friday.

Peter Townsend	What?! But your boss, Mr J. Williams, invited me to an interview!
Jenny Williams	Forget the interview. J. Williams – that's me, Jenny Williams. The boss. Goodbye.

A 2.8 **Unit 6   Ask Aysha**

Aysha	Hi again. You're listening to KFM's express phone-in show, *Ask Aysha*. Our topic tonight is *What job should I do?* And here's our next caller, Sally from Rochdale. Hi, Sally. How can I help you?
Sally	Well, er, I'm really interested in cars. My parents say I should look for office work. I've worked in an office before, in the school holidays. But I really want to be a car mechanic. But everybody says only boys can be car mechanics. What should I do?
Aysha	Don't listen to them, Sally. Boys and girls can do the same jobs. You are you. Do what you're good at.
Sally	OK. Thanks, Aysha.
Aysha	And our next caller, please. It's Greg, isn't it?
Greg	That's right. Hi, Aysha.
Aysha	What kind of job are you looking for, Greg?
Greg	I don't know. I'm not really interested in anything – except watching TV. Seriously, I love watching shows about real people. The clothes that people wear! Did you see "The Lunch Show" yesterday? That man in the green shirt and orange trousers? I mean you really shouldn't wear …
Aysha	Stop! Stop! Listen to yourself. You ARE interested in something – clothes! Look for a job at a fashion shop or department store or …
Greg	I've never thought about that before. You're right! Thanks, Aysha.
Aysha	And our next caller is Paula. She wants to be a chef. Right, Paula?
Paula	Hi, Aysha. That's right. But there's a problem. I can't cook and …
Aysha	Sorry, you want to be a chef, but you can't cook? That IS a problem.
Paula	No, well, what I mean is, I can't cook AND talk at the same time. I can only cook. People love my meals. I just can't explain things like the famous TV chefs.
Aysha	But that's fine, Paula. Forget the talking – just do the cooking. Let's take another music break …

A 2.9 **Unit 7   Going abroad for work**

Nils	Hi. This is Nils Weber. Who's speaking, please?
Sandra	Hi, Nils. This is Sandra, Sandra Jones from Ferguson's Hotel and Restaurant. I just wanted to find out if our new chef has arrived safely in England.
Nils	Good morning, Sandra. That's nice of you to phone. Everything is fine, thanks. I've just arrived in Dover. I'm still on the ship at the moment. I think I'm going to have breakfast somewhere before I start the long drive up to Manchester.
Sandra	I see. Great! Take your time. Driving too fast can get very expensive here. It's not like on one of your German autobahns!
Nils	Don't worry, Sandra. I'm going to drive nice and slowly. And I'm going to stop a few times on the way up to you. My Navi … er … my satnav says it's going to take five hours to drive from Dover to Manchester.
Sandra	It's going to take you longer than five hours today, I'm afraid. But you have a free day tomorrow and you aren't going to start work here till Monday, so it doesn't really matter.
Nils	Really? I'm glad to hear that. I'm going to listen to English radio and enjoy the drive.
Sandra	That sounds good. So you're going to arrive some time this evening. If it's past six o'clock, you'll find us in the restaurant. Just come there for the key to your flat – and for a meal, of course.
Nils	OK. I'm going to go down to the car deck now.
Sandra	Sure. One more thing, Nils. When you leave the port of Dover there's a big sign. Please read it carefully.
Nils	A big sign? What does it say?
Sandra	Links fahren.
Nils	Don't worry, Sandra! Natürlich werde ich links fahren! Of course I'm going to drive on the left! See you tonight then.
Sandra	Good luck. Bye.

1 Das *simple present*

A Allgemein

Das *simple present* verwende ich:
- um zu sagen,
  was ich regelmäßig mache.
- um zu sagen,
  was gewöhnlich der Fall ist.

*I **go** to work
five days a week.*

*I **live** in
Germany.*

B Mit *sometimes, often,* usw.

Das *simple present* wird oft mit Wörtern wie *usually, normally, sometimes, often, always, never* verwendet. Diese Wörter (Adverbien) stehen immer:
- **vor** einem Vollverb.
- **nach** einer Form von *to be.*

*I **usually** get up at 7 a.m.*

*I **often** watch TV in the evenings.*

*I'm **always** happy on Fridays.*

C Bildung: Aussagen

Das *simple present* wird aus der Grundform des Verbs (Infinitiv ohne *to*) gebildet. Nach *he/she/it* endet das Verb immer auf *-s* oder *-es!*
1. An die meisten Verben wird einfach *-s* angehängt.
2. Die Endung *-es* wird bei Verben benutzt, die auf *s, ss, x, ch* oder *sh* enden (z.B. *to finish*), da es schwer wäre, nur ein *-s* auszusprechen.
3. Auch die Verben *go* und *do* enden mit *-es.*
4. Ein Sonderfall sind Verben, die auf *-y* enden: *to tidy → he tidies.*

1. to work	2. to finish
I work	I finish
you work	you finish
he/she/it work**s**	he/she/it finish**es**
we work	we finish
you work	you finish
they work	they finish

3. to go	4. to tidy
I go	I tidy
you go	you tidy
he/she/it go**es**	he/she/it tid**ies**
we go	we tidy
you go	you tidy
they go	they tidy

D Bildung: Fragen und Verneinungen

- Fragen im *simple present* werden mit *do* (bei *he/she/it*: *does*) gebildet.
- Verneinungen bildet man mit *don't* (nach *he/she/it*: *doesn't*).

Vorsicht!

Nach *does/doesn't* kommt immer die Grundform des Verbs:
*Does he work? (**!** Does he ~~works?~~)*
*She doesn't work. (**!** She doesn't ~~works.~~)*

Fragen	Verneinungen
Do I work?	I don't work
Do you work?	you don't work
Does he/she/it work**?**	he/she/it doesn't wor**k**
Do we work?	we don't work
Do you work?	you don't work
Do they work?	they don't work

Das *present progressive*

A Allgemein

Das *present progressive* verwende ich, um zu sagen, was ich gerade mache. Ich benutze es auch, um ein Bild zu beschreiben. Es wird häufig mit Zeitangaben wie *at the moment* und *right now* verwendet.

> *I'm reading* this text at the moment.
>
> *What can you see in this photo?*
> *– A hairdresser. Right now, she's cutting a customer's hair.*

B Bildung: Aussagen

Das *present progressive* wird mit einer Form von *to be* und dem Verb + *-ing* gebildet.

C Bildung: Fragen und Verneinungen

Fragen und Verneinungen werden mit den Frage- und Verneinungsformen von *to be* gebildet.

I'm you're he's/she's/it's we're you're they're	working	I'm not working she isn't working
		Am I working? Are you working? Are they working?

Verb + *-ing*: Schreibregeln

- An die meisten Verben wird einfach *-ing* angehängt: *work – working, do – doing*.
- Verben, die auf *-e* enden, verlieren das *-e*: *use – using, dance – dancing*.
- Kurze Verben, die auf einen Vokal und einen Konsonanten (außer *-y, -w* und *-x*) enden, verdoppeln den Konsonanten: *cut – cutting* (ABER: *play – playing*).
- Längere Verben, die auf einen Vokal und einen Konsonanten enden, verdoppeln den Konsonanten nicht: *visit – visiting, deliver – delivering*. (Ausnahmen: *travelling, beginning*)
- Bei Verben, die auf *-ie* enden, wird *-ie* zu *-y*: *die – dying*

Simple present oder present progressive?

This is Patrick. He lives in England. He works in a supermarket five days a week.

It's 8.30 in the morning. Patrick is going to the supermarket by bus.

3 Das *simple past*

A Allgemein

Ich verwende das *simple past*, um zu sagen, was in der Vergangenheit geschah.
Es wird häufig mit Zeitangaben wie *yesterday*, *in 1990*, *last week* und *3 years ago* benutzt.

> Cool shorts, Gary. Where did you get them?

> I bought them in town yesterday.

B Bildung: Aussagen

- Regelmäßige Verben bilden das *simple past* mit *-ed*. Diese Form bleibt in allen Personen gleich.
- Unregelmäßige Verben haben Sonderformen im *simple past* (eine Liste finden Sie auf der vorderen Umschlagseite, innen). Diese Formen (außer bei *to be*) bleiben ebenfalls in allen Personen gleich.

regelmäßig	unregelmäßig	
to work	to go	to be
I worked	I went	I **was**
you worked	you went	you **were**
he worked	he went	he was
she worked	she went	she was
it worked	it went	it was
we worked	we went	we were
you worked	you went	you were
they worked	they went	they were

C Bildung: Fragen und Verneinungen

- Fragen im *simple past* werden in allen Personen mit *did* gebildet.
- Verneinungen bildet man durchgehend mit *didn't*.
- *to be* bildet Fragen und Verneinungen im *simple past* mit eigenen Formen.

Vorsicht!

Nach *did/didn't* steht immer die Grundform des Verbs:
Did he work? (! Did he ~~worked~~?)
She didn't work. (! She didn't ~~worked~~.)

Fragen	Verneinungen
Did I work?	I didn't work
Did you work?	you didn't work
Did he/she/it work?	he/she/it didn't work
Did we work?	we didn't work
Did you work?	you didn't work
Did they work?	they didn't work

to be	
Was I?	I wasn't
Were you?	you weren't
Was he/she/it?	he/she/it wasn't
Were we/you/they?	we/you/they/weren't

Verb + *-ed*: Schreibregeln

- An die meisten Verben wird einfach *-ed* angehängt: *work – work**ed***.
- An Verben, die auf *-e* enden, hängt man nur *-d* an: *use – us**ed***, *dance – danc**ed***.
- Kurze Verben, die auf einen Vokal (*a, e, i o, u*) und einen Konsonanten (außer *-y*, *-w* und *-x*) enden, verdoppeln den Konsonanten: *shop – sho**pp**ed*, *jog – jo**gg**ed*.

- Längere Verben, die auf einen Vokal und einen Konsonanten enden, verdoppeln den Konsonanten nicht: *visi**t** – visi**t**ed*, *deliver – delive**r**ed*. (Ausnahme: *trave**ll**ed*)
- Bei Verben, die auf *-y* enden, wird *-y* zu *-i*: *stud**y** – stud**ied***.

4 Das *present perfect*

A Allgemein
Ich verwende das *present perfect*, um zu sagen, was gerade eben (oder noch nicht) geschehen ist. Ich sage damit auch, was schon einmal (oder noch nie) gemacht wurde.

B Bildung: Aussagen
Das *present perfect* wird mit einer Form von *to have* und der 3. Form des Verbs (Partizip Perfekt) gebildet.
- Regelmäßige Verben (z. B. *to work*) bilden ihre 3. Form mit *-ed*.
- Unregelmäßige Verben (z. B. *to go*) haben Sonderformen, die in der Liste auf der vorderen Umschlagseite (innen) zu finden sind.

I have (I've) you have (you've) he has (he's) she has (she's) it has (it's) we have (we've) you have (you've) they have (they've)	worked gone

C Bildung: Fragen und Verneinungen
Fragen und Verneinungen werden mit Frage- und Verneinungsformen von *to have* + 3. Form des Verbs gebildet.

Have you worked?
 Has he worked?

I haven't worked <br> you haven't worked <br> he/she/it hasn't worked <br> we/you/they haven't worked

5 Das Futur: *will*

A Allgemein
Ich verwende *will*, um zu sagen, was ich in der Zukunft tun werde.

I'll have a family in 10 years.
 She won't leave her job when she has a family.

B Bildung
- **Aussagen** werden mit *will* + Grundform des Verbs gebildet. Die Kurzform (*'ll*) wird fast immer beim Sprechen und häufig auch beim Schreiben verwendet.
- **Fragen** bildet man, indem man *will* und das Subjekt umstellt. Hier sind die Kurzformen nicht möglich.
- **Verneinungen** werden mit *won't* + Grundform des Verbs gebildet.

I will (I'll) come you will (you'll) come he will (he'll) come she will (she'll) come it will (it'll) come we will (we'll) come you will (you'll) come they will (they'll) come	Will I come? Will you come? Will he come? Will she come? Will it come? Will we come? Will you come? Will they come?

I/you won't come <br> he/she/it won't come <br> we/you/they won't come

6 Das Futur: *going to*

A Allgemein

Ich verwende *going to,* um über Pläne und Absichten zu sprechen: *I'm going to buy a new jacket* entspricht etwa auf Deutsch: „Ich habe vor, eine neue Jacke zu kaufen."

I'm going to look for a new job next month.
Are you going to leave home?

B Bildung

- **Aussagen** bildet man mit *to be* + *going to* + Hauptverb.
- **Fragen** bildet man mit den Frageformen von *to be* + *going to* + Hauptverb.
- Für **Verneinungen** benutzt man die Verneinung von *to be* + *going to* + Hauptverb.

I'm you're he's/she's/it's we're/you're/they're	going to	work
Am I Are you Is he/she/it Are we/you/they	going to	work?
I'm not you aren't he/she/it isn't we/you/they aren't	going to	work

7 Die Verben *to be* und *to have*

A Allgemein

To be und *to have* kommen sehr häufig vor. Man braucht diese Verben auch zur Bildung einiger Zeitformen, deshalb sind sie besonders wichtig. Bei *to be* und *to have* gibt es einige Unregelmäßigkeiten, die man kennen sollte.

Are you English? – Yes, I am.
Peter has got a sister.

B Bildung

to be:

- Das Verb *to be* hat die Formen *am, is* und *are* im *simple present* und *was* und *were* im *simple past.*
- Die Verneinung bildet man mit *not.*
- Die Formen von *to be* werden oft als Kurzformen verwendet.
  Vorsicht! Apostroph nicht vergessen!

simple present	Kurzformen	Verneinung	Kurzformen Verneinung
I am	I'm	I am not	I'm not
you are	you're	you are not	you're not **oder** you aren't
he/she/it is	he's/she's/it's	he/she/it is not	he's/she's/it's not **oder** he/she/it isn't
we are	we're	we are not	we're not **oder** we aren't
you are	you're	you are not	you're not **oder** you aren't
they are	they're	they are not	they're not **oder** they aren't

simple past	Verneinung (Kurzform)
I was	I wasn't
you were	you weren't
he/she/it was	he/she/it wasn't
we were	we weren't
you were	you weren't
they were	they weren't

to have:

- Das Verb *to have* hat nur die Ausnahmeform *has* (in der dritten Person im *simple present*).
- Auch die Formen von *to have* werden oft als Kurzformen verwendet.

Vorsicht!

Die Form *have got* wird nur im *simple present* benutzt.
Die Verneinung bildet man mit *not*.
Das *simple past* von *have got* ist *had* (ohne *got*).
Die Verneinung ist *didn't have*.

simple present	Kurzformen	Verneinung *have got*
I have (got)	I've (got)	I haven't got
you have (got)	you've (got)	you haven't got
he/she/it has (got)	he's/she's/it's (got)	he/she/it hasn't got
we have (got)	we've (got)	we haven't got
you have (got)	you've (got)	you haven't got
they have (got)	they've (got)	they haven't got

simple past:
I/you/he/she/it/we/you/they **had**

Verneinung:
I/you/he/she/it/we/you/they **didn't have**

C Fragen

Anders als bei normalen Verben bildet man Fragen mit *to be* und *have got* durch Satzumstellung.
Ausnahme: Wenn *to have* ohne *got* verwendet wird, wird es als normales Verb behandelt!

Lucia **is** nice. → **Is** Lucia nice?
Tom **has got** a new car. → **Has** Tom **got** a new car?
We **had** an accident. → **Did** you **have** an accident?

D There is/are ...

Mit *there is (there's)* oder *there are* (*simple past: there was/were*) sage ich, dass es etwas gibt (gab).
Im Englischen braucht man diese Formulierung sehr oft.

There's a new club in town.
There were lots of people there last night.

8   Das Passiv

A   Allgemein:
Passivsätze betonen, **was** getan wird
(nicht **wer** etwas tut) – die Handlung steht im
Vordergrund.

> Meals **are cooked** in the canteen.

B   Bildung
Das Passiv wird mit *to be* + 3. Form des Verbs
(Partizip Perfekt) gebildet.

simple present		simple past	
I'm		I was	
you're		you were	
he's		he was	
she's		she was	
it's	made	it was	made
we're		we were	
you're		you were	
they're		they were	

They delivered oranges to the
supermarket yesterday.

Too many oranges were delivered to the
supermarket yesterday!

9   *If*-Sätze (Bedingungssätze)

A   Allgemein
Ein Bedingungssatz besteht aus einem *if*-Teil und einem Hauptsatz. Der *if*-Teil beschreibt
eine Bedingung. Der Hauptsatz drückt aus, was (nicht) passieren wird, wenn diese Bedingung
erfüllt wird.

B   Bildung
- Bedingungssätze können entweder mit
  dem *if*-Teil oder mit dem Hauptsatz
  beginnen.
- Beginnt ein Satz mit dem *if*-Teil, dann steht
  immer ein Komma vor dem Hauptsatz.

If + simple present	will (not) + verb
If you go to the party,	you'll see Mitch.

will (not) + verb	if + simple present
I won't leave Germany	if I find a good job here.

10 Relativsätze

A Allgemein

Wenn ich Sachen oder Personen näher beschreiben will, benutze ich Relativpronomen wie *who*, *which* oder *that*.

> **The woman who** is helping him is Frau Bliscz.
> **The document that** she has in her hand is Herr Krueger's letter.

B *who*, *which* oder *that*?

- *who* für Personen
- *which* für Sachen
- *that* für Personen oder Sachen

Vorsicht!

Anders als im Deutschen steht kein Komma vor *who*, *which* und *that*.

> A passenger is a person **who** travels by plane.
> A plane is a machine **which** carries people.
> Ms Brown is the passenger **that** needs special help.

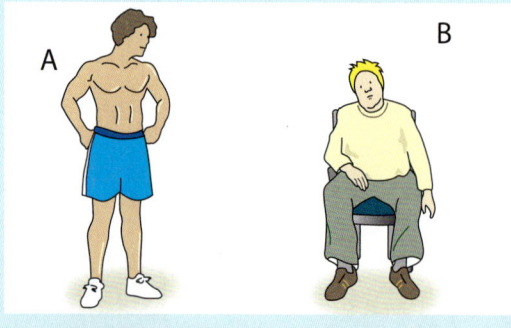

A   B

The guy who goes to a fitness club every day is A or B?

11 Adjektive

A Allgemein

Adjektive beschreiben Personen und Sachen. Sie stehen meist vor einem Substantiv oder nach *to be*.

*It is a **big** robot.*
*The robot is **big**.*

B Steigerung

- **Einsilbige Adjektive** werden mit *-er* und *-est* gesteigert.
- **Zweisilbige Adjektive**, die auf *-y* enden, werden mit *-ier* und *-iest* gesteigert.
- Bei **Vergleichen** benutzt man *than* (= als).

*Peter is **older** than Frank.*
*He is **the oldest**.*

*Susan is **prettier** than Tina.*
*Dana is **the prettiest**.*

- Die meisten anderen zweisilbigen Adjektive und alle **mehrsilbigen Adjektive** werden mit *more* und *most* gesteigert.

*John's house is **more modern** than Paul's.*
*Jackie's house is **the most modern** one in Brighton.*

*My car is **more expensive** than Melanie's.*
*Bob's car is **the most expensive**.*

- Bei **Vergleichen** von Personen und Sachen verwendet man *as … as* oder *not as … as*.

*Conny's trolley is **as big as** Frank's.*
*Sean's stereo is **not as good as** Naomi's.*

- Einige Adjektive haben **unregelmäßige Steigerungsformen**.

good	better	best
bad	worse	worst
much/many	more	most
little	less	least

*This jam is **the least expensive**.*

12 Adverbien

A Allgemein

Mit **Adverbien** sage ich, wie jemand etwas tut.

*The robot loads the lorries **quickly**.*

B Bildung

	Adjektiv	Adverb
• Ein Adverb wird gebildet, indem *-ly* an das Adjektiv angehängt wird.	quick	quick**ly**
• Bei Adjektiven mit der Endung *-y* wird das *-y* zu *-ily*.	easy	eas**ily**
• Die Endung *-le* wird zu *-ly*.	simple	simp**ly**
• *-ic* wird zu *-ically*.	automatic	automat**ically**
• Das Adverb von *good* ist *well*.	good	**well**

13 Überblick: Persönliche Fürwörter

Persönliche Fürwörter stehen für Dinge, Personen oder Tiere.
Sie ändern ihre Form, je nachdem, welche Funktion sie erfüllen.

Vorsicht!
Über einen Gegenstand spricht man nur mit *it* (nicht *he/she*).

Wer?							
I	you	he	she	it	we	you	they
ich	du	er	sie	es	wir	ihr	sie

Wem? Wen?							
me	you	him	her	it	us	you	them
mir/mich	dir/dich	ihm/ihn	ihr/sie	ihm/es	uns	euch	ihnen/sie

Wessen?							
my	your	his	her	its	our	your	their
mein	dein	sein	ihr	sein	unser	euer	ihr

14 Überblick: Besitz angeben

Eine Person ⟶ Paul**'s** book

Mehrere Personen ⟶ the student**s'** books

Sachen ⟶ the colour **of** the book

15 Gerundien

A Allgemein
Mit Gerundien spricht man über Tätigkeiten.
Sie werden wie Nomen verwendet.

Singing is my hobby.

B Bildung
Gerundien werden aus Verb + *-ing* gebildet
(vgl. *present progressive*).

Running is great to keep fit.

Videotraining: Englische Aussprache

Perfekte englische Aussprache leicht gemacht:
Mit dem Lernprogramm zur englischen
Lautschrift können Sie alle Laute einüben.
Wählen Sie einfach in der Navigation rechts den
entsprechenden Reiter (*Vowels* oder *Consonants*)
aus und klicken Sie dann auf das gewünschte
phonetische Symbol. Sprechen Sie die Wörter
laut nach.

Unter www.klett.de geben Sie einfach den
Keep Cool!-Code ein. Von dort aus können Sie die
Webanwendung online starten.

 n633sn

Keep Cool! compact dictionary zum Download
Im Internet steht die komplette Wortliste Deutsch – Englisch für Sie zum Download bereit.
Geben Sie einfach den nebenstehenden Keep Cool!-Code unter www.klett.de ein.

 em2p3f

Talking vocabulary
Außerdem finden Sie im Internet die vertonten Vokabeln der Units sowie die unregelmäßigen Verben
als MP3-Dateien zum Download. Geben Sie hierfür den Keep Cool!-Code der jeweiligen Unit bzw. den
nebenstehenden Keep Cool!-Code (für die Verben) unter www.klett.de ein.

i5ju5w

Vokabeltraining
Zum vertiefenden Vokabellernen stehen Ihnen die Vokabeltrainingseiten *Vocabulary* (S. 52 – 65)
zur Verfügung. Hier können die Vokabeln der sieben Units sowie zusätzliche Vokabeln zum jeweiligen
Thema mit abwechslungsreichen Übungen trainiert werden.

Keep Cool!-Codes

Im Internet stehen folgende Materialien für Sie zum Download bereit.
Geben Sie einfach den entsprechenden Keep Cool!-Code unter www.klett.de ein.

		Keep Cool!-Code
Units 1 – 7 Zu jeder Unit finden Sie hier – das **Talking vocabulary** – die vertonten Vokabeln der Unit als MP3-Datei – **Üben interaktiv** – Multimediale und interaktive Online-Übungsaufgaben zu den Grammatikthemen der Unit	Unit 1	f6en95
	Unit 2	45j9ub
	Unit 3	3e84cu
	Unit 4	c6x6pv
	Unit 5	s6wi47
	Unit 6	uz76gm
	Unit 7	t96aj7
Unregelmäßige Verben – vertont, im MP3-Format. Abgedruckt finden Sie die unregelmäßigen Verben auf der vorderen inneren Umschlagseite.		i5ju5w
Keep Cool! compact dictionary – die komplette Wortliste Deutsch – Englisch		em2p3f
Phonetic Alphabet – Videotraining zur englischen Aussprache		n633sn

Word list

A

abroad [əˈbrɔːd]	im/ins Ausland	42
accident [ˈæksɪdnt]	Unfall	26
ad [æd]	Anzeige	14
advert [ˈædvɜːt]	Anzeige	20
advertised [ˈædvətaɪzd]	ausgeschrieben	35
ago [əˈgəʊ]	vor	38
to agree [əˈgriː]	zustimmen	40
alcohol [ˈælkəhɒl]	Alkohol	32
all the time [ˌɔːlðəˈtaɪm]	die ganze Zeit	6
allowed [əˈlaʊd]	erlaubt	40
almost [ˈɔːlməʊst]	beinahe, fast	35
along [əˈlɒŋ]	entlang	29
another [əˈnʌðə]	ein/e andere/r/s	46
to answer the phone [ˌɑːnsə ðə ˈfəʊn]	ans Telefon gehen	8
Anything else? [ˌenɪθɪŋ ˈels]	Noch etwas?	22
anyway [ˈeniweɪ]	überhaupt	40
application [ˌæplɪˈkeɪʃn]		32
to apply (for) [əˈplaɪ]	sich bewerben (um)	32
appointment [əˈpɔɪntmənt]	Termin, Verabredung	28
apprenticeship [əˈprentɪʃɪp]	Lehre, Ausbildung	30
attached [əˈtætʃt]	beigefügt, angehängt	35
awful [ˈɔːfəl]	furchtbar	20

B

baker [ˈbeɪkə]	Bäcker/in	44
basic info [ˌbeɪsɪk ˈɪnfəʊ]	allgemeine Informationen	17
to be a team player [bi ə ˌtiːm ˈpleɪə]	teamfähig sein	35
to be able [bi ˈeɪbl]	in der Lage sein	39
before [bɪˈfɔː]	zuvor, schon einmal	37
between [bɪˈtwiːn]	zwischen	29
blouse [blaʊz]	Bluse	34
booking [ˈbʊkɪŋ]	Buchung	35
boot [buːt]	Kofferraum	26
both [bəʊθ]	beide	47
to bow [baʊ]	sich verbeugen	47
boyfriend [ˈbɔɪfrend]	(fester) Freund	13
broadband [ˈbrɔːdbænd]	Breitband	20
builder [ˈbɪldə]	Bauarbeiter/in	42
building firm [ˈbɪldɪŋ ˌfɜːm]	Baufirma	28
business card [ˈbɪznɪs ˌkɑːd]	Visitenkarte	47
to buy a round [baɪ ə ˈraʊnd]	eine Runde ausgeben	46
by the way [ˌbaɪ ðə ˈweɪ]	übrigens	46

C

cable TV [ˌkeɪbl ˌtiːˈviː]	Kabelfernsehen	20
camper van [ˈkæmpə ˌvæn]	Wohnmobil	24
canned soup [ˌkænd ˈsuːp]	Suppe aus der Dose	32
canteen [kænˈtiːn]	Kantine	13
car mechanic [ˈkɑː məˌkænɪk]	Automechaniker/in	30
car salesman [ˈkɑː ˌseɪlzmn]	Autoverkäufer	38
carrot [ˈkærət]	Möhre, Karotte	19
cassette [kəˈset]	Kassette	26
to change trains [tʃeɪndʒ ˈtreɪnz]	umsteigen	28
chauffeur [ˈʃəʊfə]	Chauffeur/in, Fahrer/in	32
chef [ʃef]	Koch/Köchin	37
church [tʃɜːtʃ]	Kirche	29
classmate [ˈklɑːsmeɪt]	Klassenkamerad/in	13
classy [ˈklɑːsi]	edel, elegant	14
clear [klɪə]	klar, deutlich	10
clothes [kləʊðz]	Kleidung	11
coat [kəʊt]	Mantel, Jacke	8
colleague [ˈkɒliːg]	Kollege, Kollegin	13
community [kəˈmjuːnəti]	Gemeinschaft	12
company [ˈkʌmpəni]	Firma	10
to continue working [kənˌtɪnjuː ˈwɜːkɪŋ]	weiter arbeiten	40
to crash the car into something [kræʃ ˌɪntə]	mit dem Auto in etwas hineinkrachen	26
crazy [ˈkreɪzi]	verrückt	14
to cross [krɒs]	überqueren	29
to curl [kɜːl]	kräuseln, aufdrehen	8
current location [ˌkʌrənt ləʊˈkeɪʃn]	derzeitiger Wohnort	17
custom [ˈkʌstəm]	Sitte, Brauch, Gewohnheit, Gepflogenheit	46
customer [ˈkʌstəmə]	Kunde/Kundin	8
CV [ˌsiːˈviː]	Lebenslauf	35
to cycle [ˈsaɪkl]	Rad fahren	25

D

to deal with [ˈdiːl wɪð]	sich kümmern um	38
to decide [dɪˈsaɪd]	(sich) entscheiden	38
department store [dɪˈpɑːtmənt ˌstɔː]	Kaufhaus	29
to depend [dɪˈpend]	darauf ankommen	34
different [ˈdɪfrnt]	anders; andere/r/s	44
directions [daɪˈrekʃnz]	Wegbeschreibung	29
to discuss [dɪˈskʌs]	diskutieren	20
to do the washing [ˌduː ðə ˈwɒʃɪŋ]	die Wäsche machen	18

to **draw** [drɔ:]	zeichnen	41
driving lessons ['draɪvɪŋ ˌlesnz]	Fahrstunden	24
driving licence ['draɪvɪŋ ˌlaɪsns]	Führerschein	26
to **dry** [draɪ]	trocknen	8

E

earphones ['ɪəfəʊnz]	Ohrhörer	8
electrician [ˌɪlek'trɪʃn]	Elektriker/in	44
employee [ɪm'plɔɪi:]	Angestellte/r	38
engine ['endʒɪn]	Motor; Maschine	38
enough [ɪ'nʌf]	genug	20
enthusiastic [ɪnˌθju:zɪ'æstɪk]	engagiert	35
Europe ['jʊərəp]	Europa	42
even ['i:vn]	sogar	38
Exactly. [ɪg'zæktlɪ]	Genau.	20
excited [ɪk'saɪtɪd]	aufgeregt	42

F

favourite ['feɪvrɪt]	Lieblings-	6
feeling ['fi:lɪŋ]	Gefühl	14
female ['fi:meɪl]	weiblich	17
field [fi:ld]	Feld	11
firm [fɜ:m]	Firma	16
first name [ˌfɜ:st ˌneɪm]	Vorname	46
flat [flæt]	Wohnung	20
we flew [wi 'flu:]	wir flogen (Grundform: to fly)	24
fluently [flu:əntli]	fließend	35
to **form** [fɔ:m]	bilden	46
friendship ['frendʃɪp]	Freundschaft	17
full-time [ˌfʊl'taɪm]	Ganztags-	40
furniture ['fɜ:nɪtʃə]	Möbel	20

G

gardener ['gɑ:dnə]	Gärtner/in	36
gender ['dʒendə]	Geschlecht	17
to **get (to …)** ['get ˌtə]	(nach …) kommen, gelangen	28
to **get off** [ˌget ˌɒf]	aussteigen	28
girlfriend ['gɜ:lfrend]	(feste) Freundin	13
to **give somebody a call** [ˌgɪv ˌsʌmbədɪ ə 'kɔ:l]	jemanden anrufen	42
glad [glæd]	froh	43
gladly ['glædli]	gern	32

H

hairdresser ['heəˌdresə]	Friseur/in	8
to **hang out** [hæŋ 'aʊt]	„abhängen"	6
headphones ['hedfəʊnz]	Kopfhörer	8
Here you are. [ˌhɪə jʊ 'ɑ:]	Hier, bitte.	22

to **hit** [hɪt]	stoßen	47
hole [həʊl]	Loch	47

I

I would [aɪ 'wʊd]	ich würde	32
I'd like … [aɪd 'laɪk]	Ich hätte gern	23
idiotic [ˌɪdɪ'ɒtɪk]	idiotisch	14
immigrant ['ɪmɪgrnt]	Immigrant/in, Einwanderer/in	44
in front of [ɪn 'frʌnt ˌəv]	vor	29
in touch [ɪn 'tʌtʃ]	in Verbindung	12
Indian ['ɪndiən]	indisch	44
instead [ɪn'sted]	stattdessen	47
interested in ['ɪntrəstɪd ɪn]	interessiert an	37
to **iron** [aɪən]	bügeln	19

J

job interview ['dʒɒb ˌɪntəvju:]	Vorstellungsgespräch	14
to **join** [dʒɔɪn]	(sich) anschließen	46
joke [dʒəʊk]	Witz	10
just [dʒʌst]	gerade, soeben	19

K

to **keep in touch** [ˌki:p ɪn 'tʌtʃ]	in Kontakt bleiben	42
to **keep your mouth shut** [ˌki:p jə 'maʊθ ˌʃʌt]	den Mund halten	40

L

language ['læŋgwɪdʒ]	Sprache	30
leather ['leðə]	Leder	34
to **leave** [li:v]	verlassen	38
look ['lʊk]	Aussehen	34
to **look after** [ˌlʊk ˌ'ɑ:ftə]	betreuen	32
to **look forward to hearing from …** [ˌlʊk ˌfɔ:wəd ˌtə 'hɪərɪŋ frəm]	sich darauf freuen, von … zu hören	32
looking for ['lʊkɪŋ fɔ:]	auf der Suche nach	17
lorry ['lɒri]	LKW	24
lunch break ['lʌntʃ ˌbreɪk]	Mittagspause	16

M

machine operator [mə'ʃi:n ˌɒpəreɪtə]	Maschinenführer/in	16
to **make friends** [meɪk 'frendz]	Freundschaften schließen	14
male [meɪl]	männlich	17
management assistant [ˌmænɪdʒmənt ə'sɪstənt]	Bürokauffrau/-mann	16
marmalade ['mɑ:məleɪd]	Marmelade aus Zitrusfrüchten	44

Word list

to **marry** ['mæri]	heiraten	38
Me too. [mi: 'tu:]	Ich auch.	14
meal [mi:l]	Essen, Mahlzeit	18
membership ['məmbəʃip]	Mitgliedschaft	14
to **mind** [maind]	etwas dagegen haben	16
motorbike ['məʊtəbaɪk]	Motorrad	24
to **move out** [mu:v 'aʊt]	ausziehen	20
mustn't ['mʌsnt]	nicht dürfen	28

N

nail polish ['neɪl ˌpɒlɪʃ]	Nagellack	22
native speaker [ˌneɪtɪv 'spi:kə]	Muttersprachler/in	35
neighbour ['neɪbə]	Nachbar/in	13
next to ['nekst ˌtə]	neben	29
normally ['nɔ:məli]	normalerweise	47
not … any more [ˌnɒt … ˌeni'mɔ:]	nicht mehr	31
not yet [nɒt 'jet]	noch nicht	26, 36

O

on the left [ˌɒn ðə 'left]	links	23
on the move [ˌɒn ðə 'mu:v]	in Bewegung	24
opposite ['ɒpəzɪt]	gegenüber (von)	29
oven ['ʌvn]	Backofen	14
over ['əʊvə]	vorbei	42
over here / over there [ˌəʊvə 'hɪə / ˌəʊvə 'ðeə]	hier / dort	22
own [əʊn]	eigene/r/s	45

P

to **paint** [peɪnt]	malen, anstreichen	22
paint [peɪnt]	Farbe	22
paintbrush ['peɪntbrʌʃ]	Farbpinsel	22
parcel ['pɑ:sl]	Paket	41
to **pass** [pɑ:s]	bestehen	8
pay [peɪ]	Bezahlung, Gehalt	16
perhaps [pə'hæps]	vielleicht	40
personal assistant [ˌpɜ:sənl ə'sɪstənt]	persönliche/r Assistent/in	32
phone box ['fəʊnbɒks]	Telefonzelle	26
phrase [freɪz]	Redewendung, Ausdruck	10
pint [paɪnt]	"Halbe" (0,568 Liter)	46
a place of my own [ə ˌpleɪs əv maɪ 'əʊn]	meine eigene Bleibe	18
plant [plɑ:nt]	Pflanze	23
to **plant** [plɑ:nt]	(ein)pflanzen	36
pleased [pli:zd]	zufrieden	38
plumber ['plʌmə]	Installateur/in, Anlagenmechaniker/in für Sanitär-, Heizungs- und Klimatechnik	44

Poland ['pəʊlənd]	Polen	44
political views [pəˌlɪtɪkl 'vju:z]	politische Einstellung	17
position [pə'zɪʃn]	(Arbeits-)Stelle	32
to **post something** [pəʊst]	etwas ins Internet stellen	12
to **produce** [prə'dju:s]	herstellen, produzieren	41
production [prə'dʌkʃn]	Produktion	16
profile ['prəʊfaɪl]	Profil, Selbstdarstellung	12
to **promise** ['prɒmɪs]	versprechen	32
pub [pʌb]	Kneipe	29
public transport [ˌpʌblɪk 'trænspɔ:t]	öffentlicher Nahverkehr	28

Q

queue [kju:]	(Warte-)Schlange	46
queuing ['kju:ɪŋ]	Schlange stehen	46

R

rat [ræt]	Ratte	20
real [rɪəl]	echt, wirklich	14
to **receive** [rɪ'si:v]	erhalten	8
to **recommend** [ˌrekə'mend]	empfehlen	34
to **register (with)** ['redʒɪstə]	sich anmelden (bei)	11
relationship [rɪ'leɪʃnʃɪp]	Beziehung	17
to **rent** [rent]	mieten	24
required [rɪ'kwaɪəd]	erforderlich	11
right [raɪt]	Recht	40
right now [ˌraɪt 'naʊ]	im Augenblick	18
right through [ˌraɪt 'θru:]	direkt durch	28
ringtone ['rɪŋtəʊn]	Klingelton	8
rule [ru:l]	Regel, Vorschrift	8

S

salad ['sæləd]	Salat	19
salesperson ['seɪlzˌpɜ:sn]	Verkaufsangestellte/r	35
salon ['sælɒn]	Friseursalon	40
satnav ['sætnæv]	Satellitennavigationssystem, „Navi"	26
to **serve** [sɜ:v]	bedienen; servieren	36
to **shake** [ʃeɪk]	zittern	20
to **shake hands** [ʃeɪk 'hændz]	Hände schütteln, sich die Hand geben	47
to **share** [ʃeə]	teilen	14
shelf, shelves [ʃelf, ʃelvz]	Regal, Regale	20
(shop) assistant ['ʃɒp əˌsɪstənt]	Verkäufer/in	22
singer ['sɪŋə]	Sänger/in	6
size [saɪz]	Größe	22
skill [skɪl]	Fähigkeit, Fertigkeit	35

skirt [skɜ:t]	Rock	34
small talk ['smɔ:l ˌtɔ:k]	Geplauder	46
smart [smɑ:t]	schick	34
smell [smel]	Geruch	20
social network [ˌsəʊʃl 'netwɜ:k]	soziales Netzwerk	12
solar panel [ˌsəʊlə 'pænl]	Sonnenkollektor	44
to **sort** [sɔ:t]	sortieren	41
to **sound** [saʊnd]	sich anhören	42
Spain [speɪn]	Spanien	24
special ['speʃl]	besondere/r/s	34
to **spend** [spend]	ausgeben	34
status ['steɪtəs]	Status	17
still [stɪl]	immer noch	18
straight ahead [ˌstreɪt ə'hed]	geradeaus	29
subject ['sʌbdʒɪkt]	Betreff	10
suit [su:t]	Anzug; Kostüm	31
to **surf the internet** [sɜ:f ði ɪntənet]	im Internet surfen	6
surprised [sə'praɪzd]	überrascht	47
Sweden ['swi:dn]	Schweden	42
Swedish ['swi:dɪʃ]	Schwedisch	42

T

to **take a photo** [ˌteɪk ə 'fəʊtəʊ]	ein Foto machen	14
to **take off** [ˌteɪk 'ɒf]	ausziehen	47
technical ['teknɪkl]	technisch	41
technology [tek'nɒlədʒɪ]	Technologie	26
test drive ['test ˌdraɪv]	Probefahrt	38
text [tekst]	SMS	8
to **text** [tekst]	eine SMS-Nachricht verschicken, „simsen"	8
that's why [ˌðæts 'waɪ]	deshalb	41
thin [θɪn]	dünn	40
through [θru:]	durch	42
tie [taɪ]	Krawatte	34
title ['taɪtl]	Anrede	11
tour guide ['tʊə ˌgaɪd]	Reiseleiter/in	35
traffic ['træfɪk]	Verkehr	46
travel agency ['trævl ˌeɪdʒənsi]	Reisebüro	35
truck [trʌk]	LKW	24
to **turn left/right** [tɜ:n 'left/'raɪt]	links/rechts abbiegen	28
to **turn on** [tɜ:n 'ɒn]	einschalten, anmachen	6

U

umbrella [ʌm'brelə]	Regenschirm	29
unfortunately [ʌn'fɔ:tʃənətlɪ]	leider	14
unusual [ʌn'ju:ʒʊəl]	ungewöhnlich	23
used [ju:zd]	gebraucht	26

V

van [væn]	(Klein-)Transporter	24

W

wall [wɔ:l]	(Pinn-)Wand	17
wall [wɔ:l]	Wand, Mauer	37
to **wash the dishes** [ˌwɒʃ ðə 'dɪʃɪz]	abwaschen, spülen	19
welcome ['welkəm]	willkommen	41
Well done [ˌwel'dʌn]	Gut gemacht!	8
What would you like? [ˌwɒt wʊd jʊ 'laɪk]	Was wünschen Sie?	23
wife [waɪf]	Ehefrau	38
the worst flat [ðə ˌwɜ:st 'flæt]	die schlimmste Wohnung	20
they would like [ˌðeɪ wʊd 'laɪk]	sie hätten gern	8
wreck [rek]	Wrack	25

Y

you should [ju 'ʃʊd]	du solltest	28
Yours sincerely [jɔ:z ˌsɪn'sɪəlɪ]	Mit freundlichen Grüßen	10

A

a/an	ein/e
a little	ein wenig
a lot	viel/e
a.m.	vormittags (nach Uhrzeiten)
about	über, um, ungefähr
across	(quer) über (hinüber)
address	Adresse
after	nach, nachdem
afternoon	Nachmittag
again	wieder
air	Luft
airport	Flughafen
all	alle/s
all right	in Ordnung
alone	allein
always	immer
and	und
angry	böse, wütend
animal	Tier
answer	Antwort
to answer	antworten
any	irgendein/e/er
apple	Apfel
arm	Arm
around	um (herum), ungefähr
to arrive	ankommen
to ask (questions)	fragen
at	an, auf, in, bei, zu
aunt	Tante
away	weg

B

back	zurück
bad	schlecht, böse
bag	Tasche
ball	Ball
banana	Banane
bank	Bank (Geldinstitut)
bathroom	Badezimmer
to be, (was, been)	sein
beautiful	schön
because	weil
bed	Bett
bedroom	Schlafzimmer
before	vor, bevor
to begin, (began, begun)	anfangen, beginnen
beginning	Anfang, Beginn
behind	hinter
big	groß
bike	Fahrrad
bird	Vogel
birthday	Geburtstag

black	schwarz
blue	blau
boat	Boot
body	Körper
book	Buch
bored	gelangweilt
boring	langweilig
bottle	Flasche
box	Karton, Schachtel
boy	Junge
bread	Brot
to break, (broke, broken)	(zer)brechen, kaputt machen
breakfast	Frühstück
to bring, (brought, brought)	bringen
brother	Bruder
brown	braun
building	Gebäude
bus, busses	Bus, Busse
business	Geschäft
busy	beschäftigt
but	aber
to buy, (bought, bought)	kaufen
by	durch, mit

C

cake	Kuchen
call	Anruf
to call	(an)rufen, nennen, heißen
can	können
cannot (can't)	nicht können
cap	Kappe
car	Auto
card	Karte
careful	vorsichtig
to carry	tragen
cat	Katze
to catch, (caught, caught)	fangen
centimetre	Zentimeter
centre	Zentrum, Mitte
chair	Stuhl
to change	ändern, verändern
cheap	billig
to check	(über)prüfen, kontrollieren
cheese	Käse
chicken	Hähnchen
child, children	Kind, Kinder
chocolate	Schokolade
Christmas	Weihnachten
cigarette	Zigarette
city	Stadt

class	(Schul)Klasse
classroom	Klassenzimmer
clean	sauber
to clean	reinigen, putzen
clever	klug, schlau, clever
clock	Uhr
closed	geschlossen
coach	Reisebus; Trainer/in
coffee	Kaffee
cold	kalt
colour	Farbe
to come, (came, come)	kommen
cook	Koch, Köchin
to cook	kochen
correct	korrekt, richtig
to correct	korrigieren
to cost, (cost, cost)	kosten
could	könnte/n, konnte/n
country	Land
cousin	Cousin/e
cow	Kuh
to cry	weinen
cup	Tasse
cut	Schnitt
to cut, (cut, cut)	schneiden

D

dad	Papa
dance	Tanz
to dance	tanzen
dangerous	gefährlich
date	Datum, Zeitpunkt, Verabredung
daughter	Tochter
day	Tag
dead	tot
dear	lieb
deep	tief
desk	Schreibtisch
to die	sterben
difficult	schwierig, schwer
dinner	Abendessen
dirty	schmutzig
discussion	Gespräch, Diskussion
to do, (did, done)	machen, tun
doctor	Arzt, Ärztin
dog	Hund
door	Tür
down	(nach) unten
to download	herunterladen
dream	Traum
to dream	träumen
dress	Kleid
drink	Getränk

to drink, (drank, drunk)	trinken
to drive, (drove, driven)	fahren
driver	Fahrer/in
dry	trocken

E

ear	Ohr
early	früh
easy	leicht
to eat, (ate, eaten)	essen
empty	leer
to empty	leeren
end	Ende, Schluss
to end	(be)enden
England	England
English	englisch
evening	Abend
every	jede/r/s
everybody	jeder, alle
everything	alles
exact	genau
exam	Prüfung
example	Beispiel
exciting	aufregend, spannend
exercise	Übung
expensive	teuer
to explain	erklären
eye	Auge

F

face	Gesicht
fall	Sturz
to fall, (fell, fallen)	fallen
false	falsch
family	Familie
famous	berühmt
fantastic	fantastisch
fast	schnell
fat	dick, fett
father	Vater
to feel, (felt, felt)	fühlen
film	Film
to find, (found, found)	finden
fine	fein, schön, gut
finger	Finger
to finish	beenden, aufhören
first	erste/r/s, zuerst
fish	Fisch
to fish	fischen
flower	Blume
food	Essen, Nahrung, Lebensmittel

Basic vocabulary

foot, feet	Fuß, Füße		to help	helfen
football	Fußball		here	hier
for	für		high	hoch
to forget, (forgot, forgotten)	vergessen		hobby	Hobby
			holiday	Urlaub, Ferien
form	Form		home	Zuhause
to form	formen, gestalten		at home	zu Hause
free	frei, kostenlos		homework	Hausaufgaben
friend	Freund/in		hope	Hoffnung
friendly	freundlich		to hope	hoffen
from	von, aus		horse	Pferd
fruit	Obst, Frucht		hospital	Krankenhaus
full (of)	voll (von, mit)		hot	heiß, scharf
fun	Spaß		hotel	Hotel
funny	lustig, komisch		hour	Stunde
			house	Haus
			how	wie
G			how much	wie viel
game	Spiel		how old	wie alt
garage	Autowerkstatt, Garage		hungry	hungrig
garden	Garten			
to get, (got, got)	bekommen, erhalten, werden		**I**	
to get up	aufstehen		ice cream	Eiskrem
girl	Mädchen		idea	Idee, Vorstellung
to give, (gave, given)	geben		if	wenn, falls, ob
			ill	krank
glass	Glas		important	wichtig
to go, (went, gone)	gehen, fahren		in	in
good	gut		information	Informationen
goodbye	auf Wiedersehen		interest	Interesse
grandfather	Großvater		interesting	interessant
grandmother	Großmutter		into	in (… hinein)
grass	Gras		to invite (for)	einladen (zu)
great	groß, großartig			
green	grün		**J**	
group	Gruppe		jacket	Jacke
to grow (grew, grown)	wachsen		jeans	Jeans
			job	Arbeit, Beruf, Job
			just	gerade, soeben
H				
hair	Haar		**K**	
half	halb		to keep, (kept, kept)	(be)halten, aufbewahren
hand	Hand			
to happen	passieren, geschehen		to kick	kicken, treten
happy	glücklich		kid	Kind; Jugendliche/r
to hate	hassen		to kill	töten, umbringen
to have (got), (had, had)	haben		kilo(gramme)	Kilo(gramm)
			kilometre	Kilometer
to have to	müssen		kiss	Kuss
head	Kopf		to kiss	küssen
to hear, (heard, heard)	hören		kitchen	Küche
			to know, (knew, known)	wissen, kennen
heavy	schwer			
hello	hallo			
help	Hilfe			

L

last	letzte/r/s
late	spät
to laugh	lachen
to learn	lernen
left	links; übrig
lesson	Unterrichtsstunde
to let (let, let)	lassen
letter	Brief; Buchstabe
to lie (down)	(sich hin)legen, liegen
life, lives	Leben
light	hell, leicht
light	Licht, Lampe
like	wie
to like	mögen
line	Linie, Zeile
list	Liste
to listen (to)	(zu)hören
litre	Liter
little	klein, wenig
to live	leben, wohnen
living room	Wohnzimmer
lonely	einsam
long	lang
look	Blick
to look	schauen, (aus)sehen
loud	laut
love	Liebe
to love	lieben
lucky	glücklich
lunch	Mittagessen

M

machine	Maschine, Gerät, Automat
magazine	Zeitschrift
to make, (made, made)	machen, herstellen
man, men	Mann, Männer; Mensch
many	viele
map	Landkarte, Karte
to match	zuordnen
to mean (meant, meant)	meinen; bedeuten
to meet (met, met)	treffen; kennen lernen
metal	Metall
metre	Meter
middle	Mitte; mittlere/r/s
milk	Milch
minute	Minute
mistake	Fehler
mobile (phone)	Handy, Mobiltelefon
modern	modern
(at the) moment	(im) Moment

money	Geld
month	Monat
more	mehr
morning	Morgen
most	meiste/r/s, die meisten
mother	Mutter
mountain	Berg
mouth	Mund
much	viel
mum	Mama, Mutter
music	Musik
must	müssen

N

name	Name
to need	brauchen, benötigen
nervous	nervös, ängstlich
never	nie(mals)
new	neu
news	Nachricht/en, Neuigkeit
newspaper	Zeitung
next	nächste/r/s
nice	nett, schön, hübsch, gut
night	Nacht
no	kein/e; nein
nobody	niemand
not	nicht
nothing	nichts
now	jetzt
number	Zahl, Nummer

O

o'clock	Uhr (Zeitangabe)
of	von, aus, bei
of course	natürlich
off	aus, weg, von
to offer	anbieten
offer	Angebot
office	Büro
often	oft, häufig
old	alt
on	auf; an-, eingeschaltet
one	ein/e/er
only	nur, erst
open	offen, geöffnet
to open	öffnen
opposite	Gegenteil
or	oder
order	Bestellung, Befehl; Reihenfolge
to order	bestellen, befehlen
to organize	ordnen; organisieren
other	andere/r/s
out	aus
over	mehr als, über

Basic vocabulary

P

p.m.	nachmittags (nach Uhrzeiten)
to pack	packen, einpacken
page	Seite
pair	Paar
paper	Papier
parents	Eltern
park	Park
to park	parken
parking	Parken
partner	Partner/in
party	Party
passenger	Passagier/in, Fahrgast
pay	Lohn, Bezahlung
to pay, (paid, paid)	(be)zahlen
pen	Stift, Füller
pencil	Bleistift
people	Leute, Volk
person	Person
phone	Telefon
to phone	anrufen, telefonieren
photo(graph)	Foto
to pick	aussuchen, wählen
picture	Bild
pig	Schwein
pink	rosa, pink
place	Platz, Ort, Stelle
plan	Plan
to plan	planen
plane	Flugzeug
plastic	(aus) Plastik
play	Theaterstück
to play	spielen
player	Spieler/in
please	bitte
pocket	Tasche
police	Polizei
police officer	Polizist/in
policeman	Polizist
polite	höflich
poor	arm
popular	beliebt
post office	Post
postcard	Postkarte
potato	Kartoffel
power	Macht; Stärke
present	Geschenk
press	Presse
to press	drücken, pressen
price	Preis
problem	Problem
programme	Programm
to pronounce	aussprechen
to pull	ziehen

pupil	Schüler/in
to push	schieben, stoßen
to put, (put, put)	setzen, stellen, legen
to put on	anziehen, auftragen, aufsetzen

Q

question	Frage
quick	schnell
quiet	ruhig

R

radio	Radio
rain	Regen
to rain	regnen
rainy	regnerisch
to read, (read, read)	lesen
ready	fertig, bereit
really	wirklich, eigentlich
red	rot
to relax	(sich) entspannen
to remember	sich erinnern an, daran denken
to repair	reparieren
report	Bericht
to report	berichten
rest	Rest, Ruhe
restaurant	Restaurant
rich	reich
to ride, (rode, ridden)	reiten, fahren
to ride a bike	Rad fahren
right	richtig, rechts
ring	Ring, Anruf
to ring, (rang, rung)	klingeln, anrufen
river	Fluss
road	Straße
room	Zimmer, Raum, Platz
round	rund
to run, (ran, run)	laufen, rennen

S

sad	traurig
safe	sicher
same	der-/die-/dasselbe, gleiche/r/s
sand	Sand
to say, (said, said)	sagen
school	Schule
sea	Meer
second	Sekunde
second	zweite/r/s
to see, (saw, seen)	sehen, verstehen
to sell, (sold, sold)	verkaufen
to send, (sent, sent)	schicken, senden
sentence	Satz
sheep	Schaf, Schafe

ship	Schiff
shirt	Hemd
shoe	Schuh
shop	Geschäft, Laden
shop assistant	Verkäufer/in
shopping	Einkaufen
short	kurz
to shout	laut rufen, schreien
show	Ausstellung, Vorstellung, Show
to show, (showed, shown)	zeigen
side	Seite
to sing, (sang, sung)	singen
single	einzel/n
sister	Schwester
to sit, (sat, sat)	sitzen
sleep	Schlaf
to sleep, (slept, slept)	schlafen
slow	langsam
small	klein
to smile	lächeln
smoke	Rauch
to smoke	rauchen
so	so
sock	Socke
soft	weich
some	einige, etwas
somebody	jemand
something	etwas
sometimes	manchmal
son	Sohn
song	Lied
soon	bald
(I'm) sorry	tut mir leid, Entschuldigung
soup	Suppe
to speak, (spoke, spoken)	sprechen
sport	Sport
to stand, (stood, stood)	stehen
start	Anfang
to start	anfangen, beginnen
station	Bahnhof
to stay	bleiben; übernachten
stop	Halt
to stop	beenden, anhalten, aufhören
story	Geschichte
street	Straße
strong	stark
stupid	dumm
subject	(Schul-)Fach
suddenly	plötzlich

summary	Zusammenfassung
summer	Sommer
sun	Sonne
supermarket	Supermarkt
sure	sicher
surprise	Überraschung
to swim, (swam, swum)	schwimmen

T

table	Tisch, Tabelle
to take, (took, taken)	nehmen, brauchen, dauern
to talk	reden, sprechen
taxi	Taxi
tea	Tee
to teach, (taught, taught)	unterrichten
teacher	Lehrer/in
to tell, (told, told)	erzählen, sagen
terrible	schrecklich, furchtbar
test	Test, Klassenarbeit
text	Text
than	als
to thank	(sich) bedanken
that (one)	der/die/das da
that	dass
the	der/die/das
theatre	Theater
then	dann
there	dort, da
there are/is	es gibt, es sind/ist
these	diese
thing	Ding, Sache
to think, (thought, thought)	denken, glauben, meinen
this	diese/r/s
those	jene
ticket	Fahr-, Eintrittskarte
time	Zeit
tip	Tipp
tired	müde
to	zu, nach; an; bis
today	heute
together	zusammen
toilet	Toilette, WC
tomato	Tomate
tomorrow	morgen
too	auch; zu
top	Spitze
tourist	Tourist/in
town	Stadt
toy	Spielzeug
train	Zug

to **train**	trainieren
to **translate**	übersetzen
to **travel**	reisen, fahren
tree	Baum
trip	Reise
trouble	Ärger
true	wahr, richtig, echt
to **try**	versuchen, (aus)probieren
TV	Fernsehen, Fernseher, Fernsehapparat

U

uncle	Onkel
under	unter
to **understand,** (**understood, understood**)	verstehen
until	bis
to **use**	benutzen, verwenden
usually	meistens, gewöhnlich

V

very	sehr
visit	Besuch
to **visit**	besuchen

W

to **wait (for)**	warten (auf)
to **wake up**	aufwachen
to **walk**	gehen, laufen, spazieren
to **want**	wollen
warm	warm
to **wash**	waschen
to **watch**	beobachten, zuschauen
water	Wasser
way	Weg
to **wear (wore, worn)**	tragen, anziehen
weather	Wetter
week	Woche
weekend	Wochenende
well	gut, gesund; also
what	was
what about …	was ist mit …
when	wann
when	als; wenn
where	wo(hin)
which	welche/r/s
white	weiß
who	wer, wem, wen
whole	ganz
why	warum
will ('ll)	werden
to **win, (won, won)**	gewinnen

window	Fenster
winter	Winter
with	mit
without	ohne
woman, women	Frau, Frauen
word	Wort
work	Arbeit
to **work**	arbeiten
world	Welt
to **write, (wrote, written)**	schreiben
to **write down**	aufschreiben
wrong	falsch

Y

year	Jahr
yellow	gelb
yes	ja
yesterday	gestern
young	jung

Z

zoo	Zoo

Bildquellennachweis

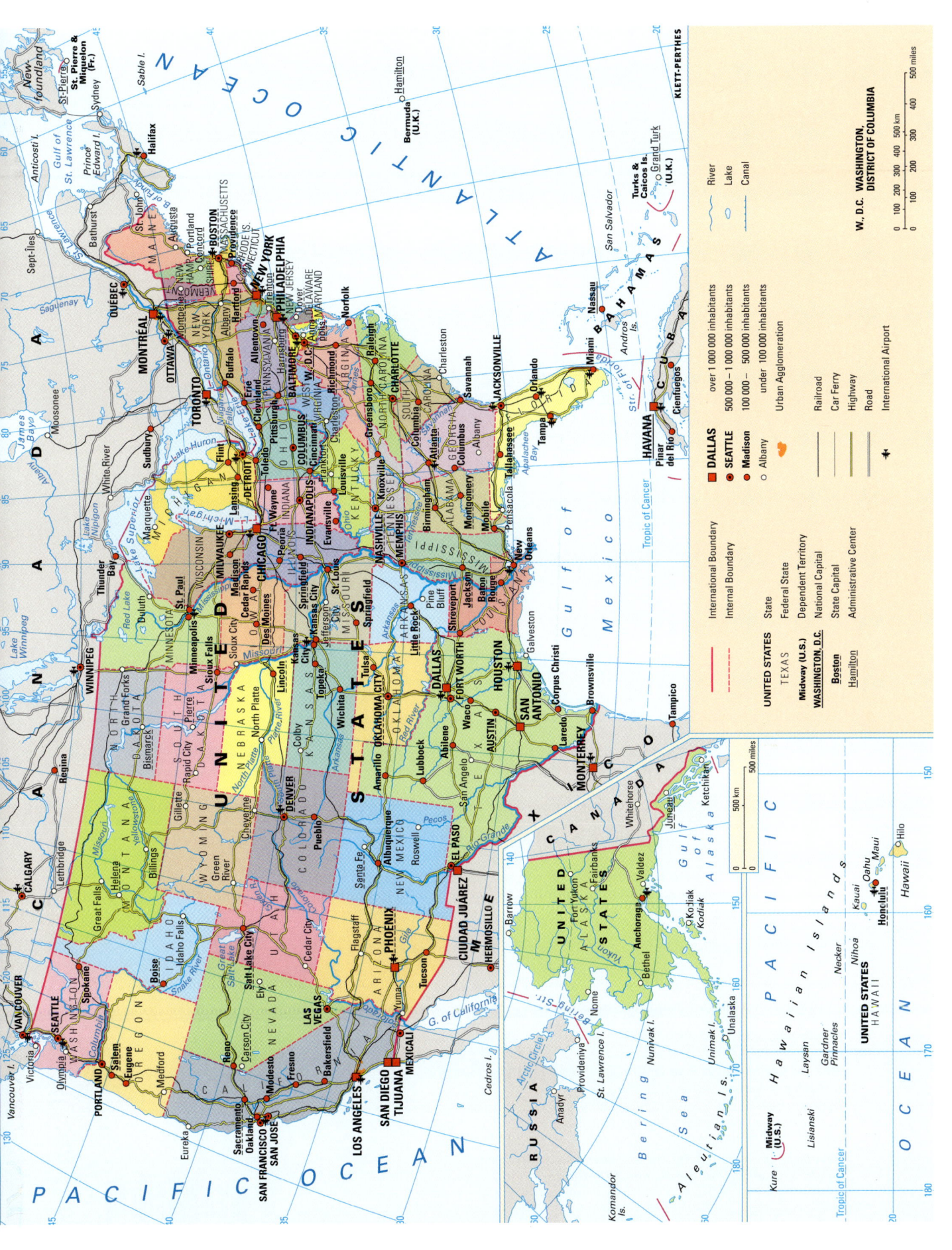

Keep Cool!
Berufsvorbereitung Englisch

von: Birgit Herrmann, Freudenstadt; Andrew K. Johnson, Cambridge
Beratung: Eva Eitel, Schwaigern; Michael Hack, Nürtingen; Tanja Weidemann, Hannover

Werkübersicht:

Cool! Lehr-/Arbeitsbuch, 978-3-12-808110-6
Keep Cool! Lehr-/Arbeitsbuch, 978-3-12-808113-7
Cool! / Keep cool! Lehrerhandbuch, 978-3-12-808112-0
Online-Ergänzungen unter www.klett.de/online

1. Auflage   1 15 14 13 12 11 | 29 28 27 26 25

Projektleitung: Matthias Rupp
Redaktion: Astrid Keller
Herstellung: Angelika Lindner

Satz und Gestaltung: B2 Büro für Gestaltung, Andreas Staiger, Stuttgart
Umschlaggestaltung: Stefanie Kaufhold, Berlin
Illustrationen: B2 Büro für Gestaltung, Andreas Staiger, Stuttgart; Jeongsook Lee, Heidelberg; Sven Palmowski, Barcelona; Chris Veit, Stuttgart

Reproduktion: Meyle + Müller Medien-Management, Pforzheim
Druck: AZ Druck und Datentechnik GmbH Kempten / Allgäu

Printed in Germany
ISBN 978-3-12-808113-7